TENSIONS IN THE CONNECTION

Into Our Third Century Series

The Church in a Changing Society, William E. Ramsden
Images of the Future, Alan K. Waltz
In Praise of Learning, Donald B. Rogers
Women, Change, and the Church, Nancy J. Van Scoyoc
Shaping the Congregation, Robert L. Wilson
Ministries Through Non-Parish Institutions,
    William E. Ramsden
Sources and Shapes of Power,
    John R. Sherwood and John C. Wagner
Context for Discovery, Neal F. Fisher
Paths to Transformation,
    Kristine M. Rogers and Bruce A. Rogers
A Practical Vision of Christian Unity, Jean Caffey Lyles
From Every Nation Without Number, Roy I. Sano
Called to Minister, Joan A. Hunt and Richard A. Hunt
Money in the Church, Joe W. Walker
Continuation or Transformation? Earl D. C. Brewer
Committed Locally—Living Globally, J. Harry Haines
Tensions in the Connection, R. Sheldon Duecker
To Proclaim the Faith, Alan K. Waltz

TENSIONS IN THE CONNECTION

R. SHELDON DUECKER

Alan K. Waltz, Editor

ABINGDON PRESS — Nashville

TENSIONS IN THE CONNECTION

*Copyright © 1983 by the General Council on
Ministries of The United Methodist Church*

All rights reserved.
No part of this book may be reproduced in any manner whatsoever without written permission of the publisher except brief quotations embodied in critical articles or reviews. For information address Abingdon Press, Nashville, Tennessee

Library of Congress Cataloging in Publication Data

DUECKER, R. SHELDON (ROBERT SHELDON), 1926–
  Tensions in the connection.
  (Into our third century)
  Includes bibliographical references.
  1. United Methodist Church (U.S.)—Government.
I. Title.   II. Series.
BX8382.2.Z5D83   1983   262'.076   82-22802

ISBN 0-687-41243-9

MANUFACTURED BY THE PARTHENON PRESS AT
NASHVILLE, TENNESSEE, UNITED STATES OF AMERICA

Acknowledgments

A brief acknowledgment of the assistance of many people in providing information, counsel, and criticism during the writing of this book cannot express adequately my appreciation for them and their contributions. Even this acknowledgment must be selective in listing names.

Those to whom I am especially indebted are:

The administration and library staff of Garrett-Evangelical Theological Seminary for their assistance during my library research;

The members of a panel which provided counsel, criticism, and direction—John Humphrey, Douglas Johnson, Leonard Miller, Norman Shawchuck, John Wagner, Alan K. Waltz, and Robert Wilson;

Bishop James Armstrong of the Indiana Area who gave encouragement, insights, and freed the time for me to complete the project;

The pastors and laypersons of the Fort Wayne District who patiently and caringly bore with me through the project;

Alan K. Waltz, editor of the series, who assisted at each phase of the project;

And my wife, Marjorie, who gave loving support and wise counsel throughout this effort and willingly gave up a vacation and other personal time together so that this project might be completed.

My hope is the book will be helpful in discussions which will lead to creative adjustments in the government and structure of United Methodism.

Contents

FOREWORD / 9

CHAPTER 1 / 13
Introduction

CHAPTER 2 / 29
Itinerant Clergy

CHAPTER 3 / 52
Decision Making

CHAPTER 4 / 76
Leadership

CHAPTER 5 / 96
Evaluation

CHAPTER 6 / 113
The Spirit of United Methodism

NOTES / 123

Foreword

In 1984 The United Methodist Church will observe its two hundredth anniversary. The Christmas Conference of 1784 is most often regarded as the formal beginning of the Methodist movement in the United States. This historic meeting adopted the Articles of Religion, established a polity, elected Thomas Coke and Francis Asbury as superintendents, consecrated Asbury at the hands of Philip Otterbein and others, took other organizational steps, and called for a rebirth of evangelism and scriptural holiness in the new nation.

The observance of the bicentennial of The United Methodist Church is a time when we pause to reflect how the Wesleyan vision of holy love and vital piety spread throughout the nation. In the report of the Bicentennial Planning Committee, approved at the 1980 General Conference, we have these words: "As we approach the end of our second century, we look forward with excitement and hope to the beginning of a third century in the service of our Lord. Our concern is that, through our recognition of the past and our affirmation of the present, we will be called into the future as new beings, refreshed by our experience of Christ, revived in our commitments to bring salvation, peace and justice to all of God's children, and renewed as a people of God in our own time."

The occasion of the bicentennial is a time to anticipate soberly the future and to assess ourselves carefully as we move into our third century. Our inheritance is one of many great achievements. We have seen periods of great expansion in our denomination, and we are now experiencing a time of contraction and entrenchment. Yet the challenge and vision are still present—to serve in the name of Christ and to spread the call to salvation and spiritual rebirth. We need to experience anew the sense of mission and purpose that filled our predecessors with the power to evangelize a nation.

Again, we turn to the words of the report of the Bicentennial Planning Committee to the General Conference: "The future is a time for new birth, and our Bicentennial prayer will be a call to new birth of the fervent spirit of Methodism, to a new birth of personal obedience to the Christ, to a new birth of creative local congregations, to a new birth of evangelical zeal, and to a new birth of vital commitment to peace and social justice."

You, as a United Methodist lay member or pastor, and your congregation have a significant role in both the search for and the celebration of a new birth in our denomination. You can help make it possible. It is the people in the pews and pulpits of United Methodism who must reestablish our identity and purpose and infuse it with the excitement and commitment to bring its mission to fruition. We believe that, through the thorough examination of who we are as United Methodists, what we want to accomplish, and how we choose to pursue our goals, we will find the renewed purpose and vision to complete our task in the name of Christ.

Into Our Third Century, a series of books initiated by

FOREWORD

the General Council on Ministries with the encouragement of the Council of Bishops, is intended to assist your reflection on and discussion of the issues confronting The United Methodist Church. The books have been based on individually commissioned studies and research projects. Over a four-year period, beginning in 1980, seventeen separate volumes are being released. The present book, *Tensions in the Connection,* is the sixteenth in the series. Books published to date are listed opposite the title page. The last book in the series will draw upon the insights gained in the series and focus on the potential for The United Methodist Church in its third century. This concluding volume will be designed for use and study in local church classes, organizations, and discussion groups.

The General Council on Ministries is pleased to commend to you this book by R. Sheldon Duecker. *Tensions in the Connection* deals with significant issues relating to the structure and government of The United Methodist Church. More precisely it focuses on tensions that are perceived as being present or developing around certain portions of the polity of the denomination. The author discusses the nature of the connection that holds United Methodists and their congregations together. He then explores some of the pressures that are coming to bear on key aspects of the polity. Several of these relate to the ordained ministry, the historic process of itineration, the method for making appointments, and the changing requirements of both the profession and the local congregations. He explores issues relating to authority and leadership and the impact these are having on traditional patterns within the polity of the denomination. Lastly, the author explores the role of polity in the denomination and how it can impact mission. The book deals with the nature of organizational structure and policy. But it does so in the context of helping us understand how this influences the way in which we express our faith and our commitment to action and how polity can serve either to enhance or hinder the basic mission.

Explore with the author the issues raised. Share your reflections and reactions to this book with others in your congregation. Discuss it with district, conference, and general church leaders. Your responses will also be welcomed by the members and staff of the General Council on Ministries.

Norman E. Dewire
General Secretary

Alan K. Waltz
Editor

General Council on Ministries
601 West Riverview Avenue
Dayton, Ohio 45406

January, 1983

CHAPTER 1

Introduction

Changes beget tensions. The ways in which people and organizations deal with tensions establish critical paths for the future, for tensions create possibilities for constructive change. Both society and The United Methodist Church are changing. Tensions have been building around the structure and governance of The United Methodist Church—that is, around its polity. Both the shape and mission of The United Methodist Church in its third century will depend heavily on how the church deals with its tensions today.

The purpose of this book is to identify and focus discussion on some key areas of tension in the church, to the end that these tensions may become creative forces for change in the future mission of The United Methodist Church.

"Connection" describes the special relationships existing between United Methodist members, churches, and organizational structures. While it is assumed that the reader has an adequate acquaintance with denominational structure and government, a thorough knowledge of the polity is not required to enable one to understand the issues that are highlighted and discussed.

Change is a constant process, not a bicentennial occurrence. Thus, tensions currently focusing on the polity of The United Methodist Church are not new. They appear to be the result of unique changes that have occurred in the church and in society during the last half of the twentieth century.

At the 1980 General Conference both the bishops and lay leaders recognized that there were significant tensions in the connection. While the Episcopal Address affirmed the connectional system, the Council of Bishops addressed some threats to that system, particularly those relating to the itinerant ministry.[1]

The Lay Address to the 1980 General Conference, the first such address in the history of the denomination, recognized what "seem to be well-organized attacks on the very connectional system which has made our unique style of ministry possible. . . . We call the church to confirm its belief in connectionalism which gives strength in times of change and reassurance for the future."[2]

Discussion of key areas of tension may cause more tension, but that is the price of trust in a democratic system. May our efforts help guide these tensions into creative forces for change in the future mission of The United Methodist Church.

Tensions

At five key points in our life together change is now taking place, or pressures for change are being felt. These current points of tension, while neither good nor bad in themselves, carry varying degrees of intensity and levels of importance. They need study, reflection, discussion, and appropriate response, since any one of them can create a new future for United Methodism!

INTRODUCTION

1. *Clergy Itineracy.* Every year each United Methodist clergy person must receive an appointment from a bishop. The result of these frequent changes is clergy itineracy. In four areas of clergy life this system creates problems: *(a)* whereas formerly clergy were not required to become professionally trained, today their seminary training requires them to cope with the image of professionalism; also their mood is toward becoming "settled pastors" who move much less frequently; *(b)* frequent moves create tensions within families in which both spouses pursue careers outside the home; *(c)* itineracy creates tension when the equity involved in home ownership is considered important for retirement; and *(d)* tension occurs when lay and clergy persons share in the pastoral appointment process.

2. *Decision Making.* An emphasis on local initiative and control seems to be lacking in United Methodism. Careful delineation of the powers of conferences and boards makes it difficult to initiate immediate and far-reaching changes in any program or agency in the denomination. Numerous program decisions are made by staff members of agencies in various headquarter locations. There are many who feel that United Methodism has become a bureaucratized denomination controlled by "representative" committees responsible only to themselves. In addition, there seems to be an unclear perception of the roles of General and Annual Conferences in the decision-making process. Finally, both clergy and laity wonder aloud that the general agencies seem to look on local congregations merely as places to raise revenue and promote programs.

3. *Leadership.* Current tensions result from: *(a)* a gradual shift in the leadership role of bishops, *(b)* a rapid rise in the roles and activities of general agencies

over the past century, and *(c)* increasing demands by laity for a voice and vote in areas of United Methodism traditionally reserved for and dominated by clergy. Perhaps it is time for a denominational commitment to the principle of lay control, reserving to clergy issues related to maintaining a disciplined and alive itineracy.

4. *Accountability and Evaluation.* Where does accountability lie in The United Methodist Church? Who is responsible for evaluation? Issues such as these are generating considerable tension in the denomination:

(a) The locus of the evaluation process seems to have shifted from individuals to the organization and society. While evaluation by the organization and society may be proper concerns of the church, the processes and rationale tend to create tension.

(b) Is self-evaluation effective? Some people believe it is impossible for an agency to evaluate itself objectively or to evaluate another agency without creating a meaningless formality.

(c) Finally, there is tension between those who believe the church should be an efficient organization and those who believe the church's main role is to witness.

5. *Ethos of the Organization.* The fragmented identities of United Methodism's various constituencies and interest groups raise the question of whether or not The United Methodist Church has a common ethos—that is, a "spirit which incorporates a history, an image, and a tradition." To be truly a church of Jesus Christ, a church must have an underlying ethos guiding its mission and ministry. Over the years the ethos of United Methodism has been dominant in the development of its polity. Now tensions are demanding the development of a common purpose in a pluralistic church and society and the expression of this common purpose through polity.

These are the polity issues facing The United Methodist Church today. In each of the following chapters one of these areas of tensions will be examined. May the concerns not be lost in the heat of emotion, but rather may they become a focus for mapping United Methodism's future under God.

Connection

Connection, the second key word in this book, describes the special relationship existing between United Methodist members, churches, and organizational structures. The term's long history in Methodism began when John Wesley described the preachers who were part of his movement as "those in connection with us."

In 1816, the Methodist General Conference replaced the word "connection" with "church," "community," or "itinerancy." Perhaps it was felt that connection lacked the dignity required to describe the dynamic, expanding denomination which was growing so rapidly that by mid-century it became the largest denomination in America. The term "connection," however, has not disappeared. The Constitution of The United Methodist Church refers to the power of the General Conference "over all matters distinctively connectional."[3]

Connection implies that the denomination's identity is in its wholeness rather than as a collection of local congregations. It lies between council, federation, or association on the one hand and a system requiring uniformity of belief and practice on the other.

To many laypersons and clergy the most important regular experience of the unity of the denomination is the Annual Conference, the basic body of United

Methodism.[4] *The Book of Discipline* reserves to the Annual Conference the rights to vote on all constitutional amendments, to select ministerial and lay delegates to the General, Jurisdictional, and Central Conferences, to accept, reject, and ordain ministerial candidates, and to handle all matters relating to the character and conference relations of ministerial members. (Lay members of the Annual Conference are not permitted to vote on the ordination, character, and conference relations of ministerial members.) Ministers are members of the Annual Conference, not of a local church. The official record of their ministry is kept in the Annual Conference journal. The Annual Conference also determines the number of districts and the method by which apportionments are assigned to local churches or districts.

Local church members often perceive the local church as the basic body of the connection, since this is where the Word of God is preached weekly, sacraments are administered, and persons are won to Christ and gathered into groups for nurture and outreach. In United Methodist polity, however, the local congregation is an expression of the larger church. Each congregation is considered technically to be a part of every other church.

The connectional polity of United Methodism provides a distinctive and clearly defined shared authority with a balance of rights and obligations. There is a healthy and continuing tension between freedom and conformity, rights and obligations, central and local authority. When functioning effectively, the system holds itself in proper check while the balance of rights and obligations provides mutual benefits and motivation for ministry.

INTRODUCTION 19

Aspects of the Connection

The structural connection of The United Methodist Church reaches from the Charge Conference, through the district, to the Annual Conference, and thence to the General Conference. *Jurisdictional Conferences,* added as part of the merger of three Methodist bodies in 1939, are given powers by the General Conference to elect bishops, determine Annual Conference boundaries, choose representatives to serve on general boards, receive appeals of a traveling preacher from the decision of a trial committee, and develop and administer programs as directed by General Conference.

The fundamental document that establishes the key directions and policies for organization and polity of The United Methodist Church is the Constitution. This 1968 document governs the life of the denomination created by the merger of the Evangelical United Brethren Church and The Methodist Church. The Constitution holds in proper balance the rights guaranteed to various components of the denomination and the obligations which relate to these rights. But the Constitution is not a static document. It is subject to change after approval by the General Conference and Annual Conferences. Its integrity is protected by the Judicial Council, which rules on constitutional questions and legislation included in *The Book of Discipline.*

The Book of Discipline is the formal legislative expression of the General Conference and may be amended by that body. As the denomination's printed polity, it is a center of unity for the connection. It serves as a standard for common practice. The strength of the connection can be seen in the ready acceptance and voluntary compliance with provisions of *The Book of Discipline* by most local churches.

Key actors in the connection are laypersons, preachers, superintendents, and bishops. From among the laity, those chosen for training and ordination to full-time ministry become preachers. From among the preachers some are chosen as superintendents and/or elected to be bishops. These latter become the supervisors in the connection.

The supervisory combination of bishops and district superintendents is unique to United Methodism. Bishops provide general oversight and leadership to the total work of the church. District superintendents serve both as supervisors under the bishops, and as an interface between local churches and the rest of the connection. The unquenchable spark of the connection, however, has been the preacher.[5] If the preacher is not "on fire for God" and committed to the goals of the denomination, the connection cannot function well. Thus, an indispensable force of connectionalism is a disciplined and directed itineracy of preachers for the purpose of mission.

Another aspect of the connection is the provision that all properties held by all levels of the denomination (1) be held in trust for The United Methodist Church* and (2) be subject to provisions of *The Book of Discipline*.[6] This provision makes possible the itinerant system of ministerial appointments by guaranteeing free and

---

*This type of provision is not unique to United Methodism. There are similar requirements in the Roman Catholic, Episcopal, and Presbyterian bodies. In Methodism the principle was first adopted as a Model Deed by the Methodist English Conference in 1763. The American version of a Deed of Settlement was approved in 1796. Since then only minor changes in phrasing have occurred.

unhindered use of church premises to every minister who is duly appointed.[7]

Connectionalism is further expressed by the existence of a relationship between the denomination and every person involved in any unit of the church. A layperson becomes a member not only of a specific local congregation, but also of the total United Methodist connection.[8] Ministers are members of an Annual Conference rather than the local church to which they are appointed, while bishops hold membership in the Council of Bishops rather than in a local church or an Annual Conference. In a parallel way, district superintendents are usually not appointed to the districts where they have been serving as pastor.[9]

Tensions in the system have raised questions about the connection for our time. While the connection exists to enable mission to happen, we must keep in mind that maintaining the connection is not the unique mission of the church. Our purpose herein is not to defend the connection, but to examine how the connection is dealing with the tensions it is experiencing. Our focus should not be on the structure, but on the mission it is meant to accomplish. When mission is being accomplished, structure is taken for granted. When structure seems to interfere with mission, structure becomes paramount. The United Methodist connection has helped shape a structure that has provided effective ministry for two hundred years. Does it still have enough meaning to serve as the basis for our future ministry?

Beginnings

The individual societies held together by John Wesley were voluntary associations of members of the Church of England. They were not a separate church. Their function was to win souls to be educated, disciplined, and nurtured in the faith. As the societies increased in number, leaders were assigned by Wesley to help tend the flocks. While Wesley visited the societies and held them together, the leaders, mostly laypersons, were the backbone of the system.

The essence of the organization which evolved from Methodist societies in England and America became standard by the 1800s and remains intact today. One great loss, however, is the feeling of *Methodism as a movement*. Methodism began as a movement within the Church of England—a movement which Wesley was reluctant to take outside the church.[10] After Methodism crossed the Atlantic, it did become a separate and identifiable church when the Methodist Episcopal Church was formed in 1784. Even so, it was a *movement* within the emerging culture of the New World.

American Adaptations

Because Wesley believed that Methodists in America needed oversight, in 1769 he designated assistants to supervise their work and a general assistant, Richard Boardman, to superintend them. In 1773 "the first American Conference did much to enlarge the superintending power for the General Assistant."[11]

Ordination was introduced to Methodism when Wesley ordained Thomas Coke and sent him to consecrate Francis Asbury. Both men were designated as general superintendents. Asbury changed their title to bishop in 1788. Asbury was not satisfied when Wesley continued to name superintendents for American

Methodists. He proposed the election of general superintendents by pastors of the American church. This practice was adopted by the Christmas Conference of 1784 and remains a standard practice of United Methodism.

Another American adaptation was the introduction of presiding elders (early counterparts to today's district superintendents). At the 1784 conference twelve elders were ordained and became forerunners of presiding elders. The term "presiding elder" appears for the first time in *The Discipline* of 1792.

The role of the bishops, Thomas Coke and Francis Asbury, was to provide oversight to the whole church. Coke, assisted by his British colleagues, formulated the major polity principles of the new church. It was Asbury who insisted on an enabling conference at which the preachers could decide for themselves whether a distinctly new church should be formed, what its polity should be, and how its leaders were to be ordained.[12]

Other bishops were added as the church spread across the continent. A major concern of the bishops and early General Conferences (national gatherings of the traveling or itinerant clergy) was the raising of money to sustain the itinerants and their families. The committees of early General Conferences were concerned primarily with clergy and their tasks of preaching and administering the sacraments.

The early Annual Conferences, more local in nature, brought together preachers of circuits and congregations to deal with issues facing the growing church. Their main concerns were qualifications of preachers, boundaries of circuits, and membership.[13]

Americanization of Methodist polity has been affected by the various social moods in the country during the past two hundred years. From the beginning, a healthy tension between freedom and tradition has helped shape United Methodist polity. At first the concern was to provide episcopal leadership. Then Jacksonian democracy arrived. By the end of the 1830s, Methodism, like all other denominations in America, had undergone a struggle between lay participation and clergy control.[14]

The General Conference of 1828 refused to approve lay representation in conferences and defeated a proposal that presiding elders be elected by the conference rather than being appointed by a bishop. Disenchantment among laypersons led to the formation of the Methodist Protestant Church in 1830.[15]

In 1844 the slavery issue provoked another schism which resulted in formation of the Methodist Episcopal Church, South, in 1846. The Methodist Episcopal Church continued to serve the northern part of the nation. Both denominations approved lay representation in the 1870s. From the 1820s through the late nineteenth century the authority of bishops was challenged, but was retained to become a foundation stone of United Methodist polity.[16]

Two Continuing Features

Although influenced by various social and cultural changes in America, two important aspects of early Methodist polity continue to characterize Methodist polity today. The first is lay participation in most aspects of church life; the second is clergy domination of issues of sacrament and order.

Laypersons carried major responsibilities in the early

societies since most clergy served several societies. Currently we find this same pattern in congregations too small to have a full-time preacher. These congregations, most with fewer than fifty members, are served by part-time ministers whose primary responsibilities are to preach and administer the sacraments. In these local churches early Methodist polity still exists—laity are responsible for the church. They must win souls, provide nurture, administer discipline, and collect money both for the operation of the congregation and for benevolences.

As congregations became larger and better established, and parsonages became available, there was a demand for a better trained, professional clergy. As clergy professionalism evolved, however, the minister became a full-time employee and assumed most of the responsibility of the church. A result of this trend has been the relegation of laypersons to roles in the local church under the direction of a minister. The minister has become a "manager," an "enabler," a "counselor," and a "prodder." Under these conditions, inevitably the primary responsibilities of the minister in United Methodist polity—to preach and to administer the sacraments—have been de-emphasized and demoted.

Historical Basis of United Methodist Polity

The distinctive functions of ordained, itinerant clergy in United Methodist polity have been to preach the gospel and administer the sacraments. Circuit riders and early preachers were sent into frontier settlements as soon as the first cabins were built. Their purpose was to preach, organize a group of believers, and move on.

They returned periodically to administer the sacraments and uplift the people through preaching. This was uniquely different from other prototypes of ministers—those of settled pastors who were called by a congregation and who might stay for a lifetime.

United Methodism, the denomination which began as "part church and part sect,"[17] was slow to accept the notion of "settled" pastors. While the local lay preacher, a layperson selected to preach and lead in a local area, is important to Methodism, the itinerant preachers are the ones who have been entrusted with the care and nurture of a church in the broader sense. Concern for the welfare of the clergy led to the establishment of general funds and assessments to the congregations to fund them.

Two similarly expanding and dynamic forces in the settlement of the nation were the United Brethren Church and the Evangelical Association, formed in the 1790s and early 1800s and particularly strong among German-speaking immigrants. These denominations adopted most features of the Methodist polity, creating a very close historical tie between themselves and the Methodists.[18]

The direct influence of the Methodist *Discipline* is seen in the *Discipline* adopted by the United Brethren in 1815. The first Evangelical *Discipline,* printed in 1809, was an adaptation of the Methodist book.

In spite of many pressures for fragmentation on the frontier, the unique polity of Methodism preserved the denomination's basic unity and thrust. While it was clergy-dominated and the bishops had much authority, it was also practical. Its practicality combined with dynamic preaching and urgent piety of frontier preachers to promote a Christian witness in a rough land.

When the denomination was split over slavery, polity was not an issue. In fact, the similarity in polity was one factor that enabled the two denominations to reunite in 1939.[19] While the Methodist Episcopal Church, South, was characterized by regionalism, it was at the same time aggressively expansive. Its polity was especially suited to the rather rural, non-industrial southern culture. A desire for strong leadership resulted in more authoritative bishops than in the northern branch.

The Methodist Episcopal Church, faced with an industrial order, adapted its work to urban life and development. Mobility of people in urban areas of the North resulted in the establishment of missionary societies. Its polity made possible the practicality of developing alternative forms of itineracy, and focusing resources of the church on areas of need, particularly during the 1930s and 1940s after the nation had become urbanized.

The way in which the church went about benevolence work affected the implementation but not the form of polity. Early benevolence activities of the church toward the poor and dispossessed had been individually directed and controlled. That is, congregations and circuits saw needs and took care of them. The Social Gospel from the 1880s onward emphasized the need for the church to respond to corporate needs of society. It was Methodism's evangelistic fervor and polity that served to allow General and Annual Conferences to address regional and national social issues as a denomination rather than as individual local churches.[20]

Bureaucratization of American society and business, which began in earnest in the 1930s, began to influence the way the church developed as a national entity. The business mentality of central control and "bigger is better" psychologically moved the church into the arena of bureaucracy. While mission boards for home and foreign activities have a long history in every denomination, and education has been a strong emphasis since the Sunday school movement began in the late 1700s, it was the mood of *consolidation and efficiency* which encouraged Methodism to organize its own bureaucracy.

Having considered briefly the historical basis of United Methodist polity and some of the tensions surrounding that polity today, let us now turn to a more detailed examination of those tensions.

CHAPTER 2

Itinerant Clergy

The United Methodist system has survived for many years as it was originally constructed—on the foundation of an itinerant clergy. In this chapter we will explore the historical basis of the itinerant system and identify some specific factors creating the tension.

Itineracy is a system in which clergy move from location to location under the appointment of a bishop. Two factors of United Methodist itineracy make it unique. The first of these is the annual appointment. While there is no limit to the number of years a minister may stay in a certain congregation, every minister must be appointed each year. In the beginning of United Methodism in this nation some bishops moved ministers among circuits at least annually, sometimes as frequently as every three months. In 1774, it was decided that all preachers were to be reappointed every six months.

United Methodist itineracy operates in such a way that each local church is provided ministerial leadership, and each minister is promised an appointment to a pastoral charge (one or more local churches). To operate effectively, the system requires that each pastoral charge must receive and support the appointed minister, and that each minister must serve faithfully the church to which he/she is appointed. This interlocking agreement between conference, minister, and church has been an important asset in helping the various branches of United Methodism spread across America.

A second unique factor is the guaranteed appointment for each ordained minister who is a member of an Annual Conference. Although somewhat revised in recent years, this practice dates from early days when it was essential that a local church provide a place of preaching and sustenance for clergy.

During the past two decades, many Annual Conference ministerial members have requested and been granted appointments outside normal church structures. These jobs include serving as a college or university faculty member, an executive officer for a secular social agency, a professional counselor, or in another capacity not requiring ordained personnel. While these ministers have moved outside normal itineracy, they continue to be treated as itinerant clergy because they have chosen to retain membership in an Annual Conference. While they usually negotiate their own employment outside church structures, they must report annually to the bishop, district superintendent, and conference Board of Ordained Ministry. In this way they maintain accountability to the conference. These employment situations are reviewed annually by the conference Board of Ordained Ministry and approved, upon the Board's recommendation, by the Annual Conference.

Another type of special appointment is the employment of Annual Conference ministerial members by a church agency or institution. Clergy serving in these structures of the denomination often take personal initiatives to secure changes of employment. Often,

ITINERANT CLERGY

bishops and district superintendents are informed after the new employment is final rather than being participants in the decision.

In The United Methodist Church in 1980 there were 4,163 ministerial appointments to positions other than as pastor of a local church. The number of these appointments varies among Annual Conferences. If, for some reason, a sizable portion of this group claimed its right to an appointment to a local church in a given year, severe tension would be created in most Annual Conferences. This possibility has resulted in the development of legislation to define more clearly appointment and accountability procedures for ministerial members serving in appointments beyond the local church.[1]

Components of the Itinerant System

The smooth functioning of the United Methodist system of itinerancy results from a practical polity in which responsibilities are clearly defined. However, its effectiveness depends on the quality of supervisory personnel—district superintendents and bishops. They, along with the conference Board of Ordained Ministry, are in charge of assuring the effectiveness of all components of itineracy; these are local pastors, ordained ministers, district superintendents, and bishops.

The 1980 General Conference technically removed local pastors (unordained lay preachers) from the itinerant system when it defined that system as "the accepted method of The United Methodist Church by which ordained ministers are appointed by the bishop to fields of labor."[2] Because of the continued importance of local pastors, however, in this book they are considered a part of the system.

Indeed, the first part of the itinerant system is the *local pastor,* a non-ordained individual who is either preparing for ordained ministry or a layperson wanting a place to preach the gospel in response to God's call. In Wesley's day, not all the preachers traveled circuits. Local pastors worked locally and served appointments near their places of residence and employment.

At first Wesley had difficulty accepting the idea that laypersons should be used as preachers. He was finally convinced that it was the will of God. An even more difficult problem confronted him when he was approached by a laywoman who had experienced the call to preach. His pragmatic direction to Sarah Crosby in 1761 was to "preach if you must, but don't call it that."[3]

From the first years of Methodism local pastors led societies, served as superintendents of church schools, and generally functioned as overseers to local churches when the itinerant ministers were not present. This group of laypersons was very important in the spread of the Methodist movement to some of our western states during the last century.[4]

There were nearly forty-four hundred United Methodist local pastors in 1980. These pastors are certified by a district Committee on Ordained Ministry for recommendation to the conference Board of Ordained Ministry. Ministerial members of the Annual Conference then have to approve the local pastors. Local pastors include: *(a)* persons enrolled as pre-theological or theological students, *(b)* persons who do not devote full time to pastoral work, and *(c)* persons who devote their entire life to the work of the church to

ITINERANT CLERGY

which they are appointed. Both part-time and full-time local pastors must complete annual study requirements unless they have completed the course prescribed by the general Division of Ordained Ministry. Full-time local pastors must receive not less than the minimum salary set by the Annual Conference.

Part-time local pastors generally serve smaller churches which are not able to support a full-time pastor. While the denomination is grateful for the faith, commitment, and availability of these special persons, continued dependence on their service in small congregations raises questions about the manner in which full-time pastors are deployed. Many small membership churches have had the equivalent of part-time local pastor leadership for many years. While ordained elders have not been considered as possible pastors for some of United Methodism's smaller churches, 1980 legislation providing for less than full-time service by conference ministerial members may change this.

The second part of the system is the ordained minister. The ordained ministry of The United Methodist Church is composed of elders and deacons. Elders are ministers who have completed the formal preparation for ministry, have been elected itinerant members in full connection with an Annual Conference, and have been ordained elders. Deacons are ministers who have made sufficient progress in their preparation for the ministry to be received as probationary members or associate members of an Annual Conference and who have been ordained deacons. Itinerant elders comprise the bulk of the clergy pool, devote full time to ministry, and are subject to annual appointment.

The United Methodist style of itineracy is held together, historically and currently, by the district superintendent. Historically the district superintendent was frequently the key minister on the frontier. Because there was no denominational growth strategy, it was the responsibility of the superintendent to map out circuits, help organize new churches, and secure pastoral leadership.[5] The office of district superintendent is still important in the development of strategy for the church. Today superintendents draw and establish circuit boundaries, make certain that preachers are assigned to congregations and circuits, and evaluate preachers.

The office of bishop ties United Methodists together. The bishop's roles in itineracy include presiding at sessions of Annual Conferences, ordaining clergy, working with district superintendents in the appointment of ministers to circuits and congregations, and other tasks.

Over the years itineracy has been adapted to the needs of United Methodism. Four challenges have emerged which are likely to influence United Methodism's itineracy polity: (1) professionalization of the clergy, (2) laity's desire to share in appointive decision-making powers, (3) clergy's desire to become more "settled" than itinerant, and (4) the rise of pluralism.

Professionalization

Key factors defining a profession are: required schooling or training in a specific discipline, certification by a recognized professional agency, and a code of conduct or ethics which guides the professional in fulfilling her/his vocation. While professions have been a part of society for many years, proliferation of professions is a rather recent societal development. The rise of bureaucracies not only has fostered new professions, but also has created specialties within professions. Trends toward specialization are apparent in business, industry, government, and the old-line professions of medicine, law, and education.

United Methodist clergy are professionals. While their largest category is comprised of generalists, specialization among clergy is being seen also. One reason for the increase in the number of special clergy appointments is the opportunity to specialize. For example, clergy may prepare for and serve entire careers as military chaplains, hospital chaplains, pastoral counselors, or church administrators. A source of tension for the Annual Conference and its ministerial accountability system is the relationship of these specialists to officially organized professional groups which give recognition and certification beyond those conferred by normal church channels.

The greatest change in United Methodism's professional requirements has been in the area of education. Pastoral education has always been important in the denomination. John Wesley's heritage to Methodist clergy included a strong emphasis on traditional education, which meant being able to read and write, being versed in classical languages and the classics, and seriously studying the Scriptures.[6]

Increased educational requirements have raised speculation from some in the church that today's pastor is out of touch with certain groups in society. This is not a new criticism of educated United Methodist clergy. As early as the period immediately following the Civil War it was felt that some clergy had difficulty relating to newly freed blacks, the poor, and western frontier people.[7]

More than half of the Methodist ministers joining Annual Conferences in 1939 had no training in theological schools. At that time the primary educational choice for entrance to membership in an Annual Conference was a four-year Course of Study consisting of a list of books which a candidate studied and on which he/she was examined before admittance to an Annual Conference. In 1944, the General Conference of The Methodist Church went on record favoring seminary education for ministers. Not until 1956 was seminary graduation made the normal qualification for conference membership.[8] Since then additional requirements have been added, including psychological testing and supervision of a candidate for two years before acceptance into the itinerant ministry.

Professionalization among United Methodist clergy has been strengthened further by Annual Conference programs of continuing education. Current legislation encourages leaves of absence for study at least one week each year and at least one month during each quadrennium. Many ministers also have enrolled in advanced degree programs of seminaries or universities.

These trends in professionalization have created at least three important pressures on the itinerant system.

1. The financial expectation level of professionals tends to escalate. Clergy groups frequently discuss the disparity between clergy income and that of other professionals who satisfy long-term education requirements, such as doctors. Early General Conferences collected money to assure the income of itinerants.

Providing an adequate living, however, is not the same as receiving a salary commensurate with others who have the same level of training.

2. The perception of ministry as a profession tends to influence personal goals of ministers, thus affecting the itinerant system. For example, professionals have "careers," while itinerant Methodist clergy historically have followed the "call to preach." Professionals plan their careers, while itinerants historically have gone where they were sent. A professional ministry derives its authority from the organization, while a called ministry receives its authority from God.

A 1969 study by Murray H. Leiffer suggests that motivation for entering the ministry is changing. The two primary motivations given by Methodist pastors for entering the ministry were "a distinct and divine call" and "a desire to lead men to a personal religious experience." These two factors, according to the study, were especially important to pastors forty-five years of age or older, but declined steadily in importance in the younger age categories. The younger pastors gave more importance than older pastors to such motivations as "a belief that Christianity offers the solution to the social and political problems of a disorganized world," "enjoyment of working with people . . .," and "the influence of a minister whose example I wanted to follow."[9]

These changes in motivation suggest that the historic United Methodist sense of evangelism is being replaced. Instead of evangelical witness, the denominational concern seems to be moving in the direction of trying to solve the world's problems through the church.

The professional places less emphasis on being led by the Spirit and more emphasis on a planned career with regular advancement. In this sense, itineracy is somewhat like a union which rewards the members not necessarily because of ability, but because of persistence and longevity.

3. Professionals separate themselves from nonprofessionals. One cynic says, "The professional creates a language that only another professional understands." A preoccupation of professionals is to protect their turf. While this may be important in certain kinds of occupations, it has serious limitations when applied to a voluntary organization in which the professional is required to recruit, lead, and train non-paid persons. The polity of United Methodism has emphasized a distinction of roles, but not at the expense of either clergy or laity. Laity have had some responsibility for running the congregation, while clergy have given oversight and direction, preached, and administered the sacraments. Increased emphasis on professionalization of the clergy may lead to more clergy domination of the church in the future.

Professionalization of the clergy has had a parallel movement among lay professionals, including diaconal ministers. Lay professionals, as opposed to itinerant clergy, have experienced discrimination in pensions, group insurance coverage, salary, and continuing education. Some feel that ordained ministers regard them as second class, and the functions they perform as less important than the "real" ministry.

Diaconal ministers are non-ordained persons who commit themselves to full-time ministry in The United Methodist Church after having met certain denominational standards and being consecrated by a bishop at a session of Annual Conference. One reason for the emergence of diaconal ministry has been the desire for recognition, standards, and compensation. According to a 1981 survey of members of Annual Conference Boards of Diaconal Ministry, the concern most frequently mentioned was to "bring diaconal ministry up to the level of ordained ministry . . . in benefits, recognition, and support."[10]

In 1981 there were 935 diaconal ministers. An additional 457 persons were enrolled in certification studies to become recognized as diaconal ministers. In the same year there were more than 36,000 clergy in the full, probationary, and associate member categories. While the present number of diaconal ministers is small, their availability and qualification for service in local churches will affect the itinerant system. Their certification by the denomination and the use of "minister" in their title elevates their status over other lay professionals. Their presence offers local churches a new option for staff selection. Employment of a diaconal minister allows the local church to make its own arrangements and frees it not only from the appointment procedure related to itinerant clergy, but also from having to maintain and care for a parsonage.

While tensions in the itinerant system are created by professionalization of the ministerial members of Annual Conference, more tension may be noted when the full impact of diaconal ministry is felt.

Shared Decision Making on Appointments

The presiding elder was the key actor in early American Methodism. As administrator, he supervised the circuits and attempted to meet quarterly with pastors in their churches. By providing spiritual oversight and developing growth strategy for the church, the presiding elder represented the Methodist denomination.

The need for superintendence has not been diminished. Even though the local church is self-determining in much of its ministry and mission, it is an integral part of the denomination. It is still important for the district superintendent to visit local churches in order to provide oversight and general direction in keeping with the goals of the denomination.[11]

Although the superintendent has the same kind of responsibilities as in the past, social forces are raising issues about the way those responsibilities should be met. One area of current tension is the increasing expectation and desire of laypersons to have a larger voice and vote in decisions which affect their church—locally, regionally, and nationally. This is not a new phenomenon in American Methodism. The secession of the Methodist Protestant Church in the 1820s was caused by the General Conference rejection of lay representation.

Laypersons have sought and secured more representation. They have requested and assisted in establishing a system of consultation for making appointments in local churches. They consult with the district superintendent to clarify missional needs and pastoral leadership qualities best suited for a pastoral charge. Further consultation is required before the appointment of a specific pastor. While *The Book of Discipline* makes clear that authority for pastoral appointments rests with the bishop,[12] the practice of consultation causes local church leaders to believe they do the actual hiring and firing.[13]

Laypersons have always had a strong voice in United Methodism except at the clergy supervision level. To determine the adequacy of each clergy person under appointment, the United Methodist itinerant system has depended on evaluation by the district superintendent and bishop. This method has worked and continues to work as well as, and perhaps better than, polities of most other denominations. This is another area, however, where laypersons want to influence decisions affecting them and their local church.

The mood is in keeping with the social era in which the church exists, for the same spirit pervades other public institutions such as schools. If we are to capitalize creatively on the tension, we must revise the rights and roles of laypersons and the appointive needs of the denomination to represent the current age. The question of who controls or speaks for the local church is never easy to answer.

Lay participation in appointment-making involves a small group of laity who are elected to their positions for a few years. Some of the questions that pinpoint tensions are: Can such a small group really speak for a local church? What about the non-actives who are not represented on the committees interviewing pastors? Is not the itinerant system of supervisors able to judge the needs of a congregation and the potentialities of a particular pastor?

The desire of laity to share the power of appointment-making is laudatory, but it must be tempered by the realities of taking responsibility for the results of the appointment. Historically, the United Methodist itinerant system put the responsibility squarely on the bishop and district superintendent. Including laity in appointment-making would seem to place them in the role of assuming some responsibility for the results of the appointment. While some would call lay consultation a way for district superintendents to increase the effectiveness of the appointive process, limitations imposed by a large number of churches and their committees may be more burdensome than helpful.

The evaluative system for clergy is another way in which laity are sharing power in the appointive system. Currently the local church Committee on Pastor-Parish Relations annually evaluates the effectiveness of the pastor. The district superintendent is also involved in this process. The denomination, like most bureaucratic organizations, has developed methods to rate and evaluate its staff.

The tension does not center on whether the church uses the same methods of evaluation as other institutions. The tension centers on how best to make the itinerant system reflect new roles and responsibilities of laypersons, while keeping intact the uniqueness of a system that has made United Methodism an important force in American culture for two hundred years.

Settled Pastors

The twin pressures on the itinerant system—professionalization and increasing influence of laity in appointment-making—have increased the desire of many United Methodist clergy to become settled pastors. A settled pastor remains in a community for a long-term pastorate.

The United Methodist itinerant system, of course, has favored frequent moves and shorter pastorates. Frequent changing of pastors has been a problem for the United Methodist itinerant system from its beginning. People like to have a home base. Yet itineracy demands

ITINERANT CLERGY

that pastors live without permanent residence in one community. Thus, the pastor's allegiance is supposed to be to the conference and the denomination, not a local church or community. In theory the clergy's attention is focused on the mission of the church rather than on community and family conflicts.

The issue of settled *versus* itinerant clergy has been debated within United Methodism almost from the beginning. In the early American Methodist Church celibacy was emphasized. Asbury never ceased to pay tribute to the celibate itinerant preachers, for he recognized that marriage was a pressure toward a settled ministry and, therefore, an impediment to itineracy. By 1816, however, General Conference urged societies to secure parsonages for preachers, a clear indication of a move toward a settled clergy.[14] Urbanization of the nation in the late nineteenth century required modifications in itineracy. Resident pastors were already accepted in the most populous areas of the North and East.

Less than a quarter century ago, clergy did not always know where they were to be assigned when they came to the Annual Conference sessions. On the last day of Annual Conference, usually as a last item of business or at a worship service, the bishop read the ministerial appointments for the coming year. Some clergy were totally surprised to discover they were moving. This was in the Methodist tradition of reading and fixing appointments.

The female spouse role, as redefined by society, has had a sobering effect on the appointive system. Currently more than half the married women in American society work. Since the early 1970s in many clergy families both spouses work. The salary of the female spouse had not been regarded as essential before the women's movement gained momentum in the 1970s. Today, however, many women are reluctant to give up their jobs when their husbands are assigned to a new local church. Unexpected changes in appointment are not taken lightly, if at all.

A mood of increasing acceptance of settled pastorates is evident during the appointment-making process. For example, during early consultations on a possible move, pastors show interest in church size, salary and financial arrangements, housing, education opportunities for family members, presence or absence of a secretary, and geographical location of the church. These criteria are often more important to the pastor than a willingness to be moved "wherever the bishop feels I am needed." Predictably, pastors serving large churches with higher salaries want to move less frequently. Tensions created by these new criteria are results of complex social changes. Yet the denomination must deal responsibly with pastors who assert their preference for appointments which enhance their personal status, reflect a positive image in the Annual Conference, and provide cultural and educational opportunities for their families.

A complication impacting itinerancy at this juncture is a change in the upward mobility of the system. Historically, a successful pastor expected to move to increasingly larger churches. Today that type of opportunity has been curtailed for most ministers by shifting populations, fewer new churches, and later retirement ages.

Another factor impacting the swing in mood toward settled pastorates is an increasing desire among clergy to be paid a housing allowance rather than be provided a parsonage. Although this option is now permitted in some Annual Conferences, guidelines are imposed to assure mobility within the itineracy system. The fact that some Annual Conferences have established guidelines to accommodate the clergy desire for home ownership suggests a willingness to explore further the benefits of a settled pastor concept.

Another force influencing consideration of a settled pastor concept is the presence of ministerial couples as members of Annual Conferences. If both members serve full time, limited opportunities for movement may cause clergy couples to serve longer pastorates.

At least four models of clergy couple deployment are evident: (1) each ministerial member serves a separate charge; (2) both members serve in a single charge by dividing time and responsibility but receive one full-time salary; (3) both serve full time in a single church with each receiving a full-time salary; and (4) one member serves in a church while the other serves in a special appointment with the conference or one of its institutions. Each of these arrangements, unique because of a more complicated appointment-making process, takes longer to work out and tends to promote longer pastorates for these couples.

It is likely that situations will occur where one member of a clergy couple should be appointed to a different church while the appointment of the other member of the couple should not change. Then this becomes a basic polity decision to decide between a settled pastorate or an itinerant clergy model. However, the denomination still bears responsibility for clergy couples as persons when, as ministers in the system, they experience marriage stress because of competing career choices, varying levels of professional recognition, and the need to commute to widely separated churches.

Itinerancy is also influenced by the female clergy who is married to a layperson. It appears to be even more difficult for a man to move to meet the needs of his spouse's job, than vice versa. While this may be a brief holdover from the past, those of us living in the present must address the issue.

The full impact of women clergy on itinerancy has yet to be felt. Recent studies indicate that clergy women do not receive salaries equal to male counterparts. No data are available to show whether this is because women are appointed at lower salary levels in the beginning, whether they receive smaller annual increments, or whether some local churches refuse to accept them as pastors and thus limit their mobility. The test of the church's intention to provide women equal opportunity in ministry will come at the third and fourth appointments of a woman pastor. Most Annual Conferences tend to place new seminary graduates at the same salary level. Therefore, discrimination based on sex will not become apparent until women pastors experience three or four changes of appointments.

Ethnic Minorities

When The United Methodist Church moved to become a corporate social change agent, it adopted a stance that imposes on itinerancy certain personnel expectations. One of these is equal opportunity for persons regardless of race or ethnic background. This principle is enforceable only in those parts of the system over which direct supervision can occur, such as employment by the general agencies. The church has attempted to provide opportunity for proportional representation of racial and ethnic minority persons in the membership of boards and agencies through a quota system.

The stated goal of The United Methodist Church since 1968 has been to provide equal opportunity for local church membership, attendance at worship, participation in programs, and employment for "all persons, without regard to race, color, national origin, or economic condition."[15] This concern has been addressed by every General Conference since 1968—a clear indication of continuing concern and commitment.

In 1972, General Conference legislation gave bishops the responsibility to "seek the cooperation of the Cabinet and congregations in the appointment of pastors without regard to race or color."[16] This was affirmed in 1976 with the addition that appointments be made "without regard to race, ethnic origin, sex, or color."[17] In 1980 the phrase "consistent with the commitment to an open itineracy" was added.[18]

Open itineracy, appointing clergy to congregations without regard to race, ethnic origin, sex, or color, is a commendable goal. It assumes that each preacher deserves equal consideration for an appointment. However, open itineracy today produces tensions not faced by United Methodists previously.

First, it is difficult to identify and deal with racism. Prejudices, advantages for the majority, and resultant oppression of the minority are built into personal life-styles and church systems. Since racism exists in cabinet members it is difficult for them to assess whether even-handed consideration is given in the appointment of all pastors. Fear of conflicts which may grow out of resistance from local churches to the appointment of a minister of a different racial or ethnic group may discourage cabinets from pursuing such appointments even where there is appropriate matching of leadership skills and local church needs. Racism exists in members of local churches. Awareness of this reality may cause local church leaders to refuse to accept the appointment of an ethnic minority pastor. For these reasons related to racism, open itineracy appointment-making is difficult.

Second, it is difficult to assess all the motives behind specific appointments. The purpose of the itinerant system is deployment of clergy so that the mission of the church can be achieved. Often appointments are perceived to be based on such factors as granting rewards for faithful service, punishment, or recognition of personal friendship. Sometimes bishops and cabinets are perceived as using the itinerant system to make social action statements. An example would be the appointment of a pastor of one race or ethnic group to serve a church composed primarily of persons from a different racial or ethnic group, a cross-ethnic appointment. Such appointments should be made primarily on the basis of the local congregation's missional needs, not to make a social statement. This is not to say that cross-ethnic appointments should not be made. It is to affirm that appointments, to quote Dr. Woodie White, General Secretary of the General Commission on Religion and Race, "should be made on the basis of what will enhance the mission of the church."[19]

Third, the principle of open itineracy may conflict with the growing awareness of, appreciation for, and desire to celebrate ethnicity. There is growing acceptance of the fact that some ethnic and racial identity is not only necessary but also desirable. Some ethnic groups cannot be absorbed into a dominant culture. A General Board of Discipleship book, *Ethnic Minorities in The United Methodist Church* states, "ethnicity has come to refer to those ethnic groups which are 'unmeltable'—Black Americans, Hispanic Americans, Native Americans, and Asian Americans."[20]

Distinct cultural differences cannot be ignored or violated in pastoral appointments. It is important to strengthen these groups because they provide ministry to large segments of the nation's population. In addition, these ministries enrich the life of the total church.

Cross-ethnic appointments require special pastoral leadership skills not needed in other appointments. Not only must the pastors understand the cultural differences, but also they must be quite flexible. Such appointments demand that pastors adapt to the church's cultural experience and not expect the church to adapt to theirs.

Increasing ethnic distinctiveness will occur in our nation and in our church in the near future. Expected changes include more churches where Spanish and Asian languages will be used as well as new black congregations composed of persons primarily from the Caribbean. The difficulties these changes indicate are no greater than difficulties faced previously by our church. Racial and ethnic pluralism and the goal of open itinerancy require bishops and cabinets to be sensitive to unique cultural varieties and language differences in the Annual Conference.[21]

A fourth problem of open itinerancy is lack of personnel. More churches are open to cross-ethnic appointments than there are pastors available or ready to participate.[22] Furthermore, ethnic minority pastors who want open itineracy often find it difficult to participate when the opportunity arises. They may experience pressure from their peers not to leave the ethnic church since their leadership is needed in the ethnic community. Other questions they face include: How will it look? What will it mean for my future? and What sacrifice does this mean for my family?

A fifth factor is the existence of ethnic minority caucus groups in many Annual Conferences. Some caucuses claim the right to be consulted on the admission of an ethnic pastor to the Annual Conference and a voice in the appointment of ethnic pastors. While consultation with caucuses by bishops and cabinets may be useful, caucuses should not decide the appointments. As Woodie White said, "We can't afford to have cabinets relinquish their responsibility."[23] Caucuses should not determine appointments.

Some, but not much, progress has been made toward open itineracy. In the mid-1970s there were one hundred forty-three cross-ethnic appointments in the church, all in racially stable churches and communities. Fifty of these appointments were white pastors serving ethnic minority churches.[24]

At least thirty-two cross-ethnic appointments were made in 1981, an increase over 1980. Of these, twenty-six were ethnic minority persons appointed to white churches and six were white pastors appointed to ethnic minority churches.[25]

The question of open itineracy causes some severe tensions in the connection. Few issues divide the church more sharply. Sentiment ranges from the pastor who said, "It isn't working. It hasn't worked and it's dead as a

ITINERANT CLERGY

dodo bird in this part of the country," to a conference lay leader who said, "If our faith is genuine at all it will support and bring about open itineracy."

In this chapter we have considered only some of the tensions being encountered in itineracy. There are no easy solutions, but the issues must be faced. Since itineracy and its tension spots affect every lay and clergy person, each has both a right and an obligation to become involved in finding solutions.

CHAPTER 3

Decision Making

United Methodist polity allows decisions to be made in several places. While the church's combination of hierarchical and non-hierarchical decision making may appear to be based on foresight, in actuality this diffused decision-making pattern has simply emerged.

The hierarchy is related more to the clergy than to the denomination as a whole. The bishop represents the apex of clergy structure. This is hierarchy. For church members, the local congregation is the authority. That is not hierarchy.

This dichotomy is complicated further by authority given to conferences, boards, and agencies of the church. A structure diagram or organization chart of United Methodism would not reflect an accurate picture of the denomination's internal dynamics.

United Methodists are practical people. They believe that each component of a complicated organization needs authority to make decisions for which it is responsible. Their belief, however, does not necessarily mean that United Methodists are willing to comply with all such decisions. Not at all!

It is not unusual for the decision of a conference, board, agency, or even a bishop, to be ignored and made ineffective by congregations and clergy who choose not to implement or recognize the decision as binding. The

DECISION MAKING

United Methodist Church is a voluntary hierarchical organization. This means all decisions are not made by a central hierarchy; even though various groups with authority make decisions, persons *decide* whether or not to comply.

Recent pressures for broader participation in decision-making processes have resulted in slower and less effective decision making. Since carrying out decisions is a test of an effective organization, an examination of decision making may provide insight into current polity tensions in The United Methodist Church.

Compliance in some administrative areas such as the pension plan is quite high. On the other hand, compliance with the legal trust requirement on church-owned property is sometimes done resentfully and without an understanding of its meaning. Indeed, this law of the church has been challenged frequently in the denomination's history.

While no applicable data exist, observers believe that there have been in recent years more cases of local churches challenging the property trust clause.[1] Issues which have precipitated the challenges have been the Evangelical United Brethren-Methodist union, resistance to episcopal authority in the appointment of pastors, and theological differences. In general, however, compliance with decisions made by legislative bodies and designated leaders has been good. The mood in the denomination is one of cooperation.

These observations suggest that there are times in which the United Methodist membership intentionally does not act. It chooses to do so even though it has an efficient church structure, broad representation in decision-making bodies, and decision making appropriate to the responsibilities of each center of power.

Selective compliance raises issues about decision making. First, there is no single center of power and authority in the denomination where decisions affecting all members are made. This absence of a central authority may not only confuse the membership, but also make resourcing the denomination extremely difficult, if not impossible.

Second, most decisions require voluntary compliance. No formal system of sanctions exists to penalize churches that choose to ignore certain decisions. It is doubtful whether an effective sanctioning system could be developed and implemented. On the other hand, all decisions may not require the same degree of compliance. The church, acting out of group wisdom, may offset inappropriate decisions through neglect. This is a passive way of rejecting decisions made by legislative bodies led too far from the basic beliefs and values of the people for whom they are legislating.[2]

Third, many decisions have little or no effect on most members either because they are already in compliance with the decisions or because the requests are not germane to their location or situation. Perhaps The United Methodist Church, based on its historical polity, may need to give more program control to local churches rather than lodging program development in national boards and agencies.

Appointment of the Pastor

In early Methodism, the bishop made pastoral appointments without conferring with anyone. It was not until 1804 that bishops enforced rules about the length of time a pastor stayed in a church.[3] This procedure was amended through practical necessity as the church grew and worked on the frontier. The district superintendents, who worked more directly with pastors than the bishop, became intimately involved in appointment-making also through practical necessity. Their participation was incorporated into church polity after being introduced in the early 1800s by Bishop McKendree.[4] Even though district superintendents were consulted, the bishop still *fixed* pastoral appointments at Annual Conference sessions. Like other changes relating to pastoral appointments, the innovation of consultation with district superintendents was strongly opposed.

A change made in 1940 required that the bishop "announce openly to the cabinet his appointments; and . . . before the final announcement of appointments is made the district superintendent shall consult with the pastors when such consultation is possible."[5] In effect, this resulted in the emergence of the cabinet (bishop and district superintendents) as the pastoral appointment-making body in each Annual Conference. While this change did not lessen the authority of the bishop it made official a long-time practice of bishops and district superintendents.

A requirement which became a part of *The Book of Discipline* in 1972 calls for consultation with the local church Committee on Pastor-Parish Relations before and during a pastoral appointment change. Even today, however, there abound varying interpretations of the meaning of such consultation.

To understand how much change there has been, let

us examine the current appointment-making process. Currently, the decision to appoint a pastor is shared by the bishop, the cabinet, the pastor, and the local church. Thus, while the *authority* to make the appointment is ultimately the bishop's, the district superintendent must be involved in a consultation process with the pastor and the local church.

When a vacancy occurs, the bishop and cabinet initiate a possible appointment. Only after consultation with the pastor and an elected committee of members of the congregation will the appointment become effective. This time-consuming process is a response to pressure from pastors and local church Committees on Pastor-Parish Relations who have asked for more voice in appointment-making.

In 1981, the Judicial Council was asked to clarify the meaning of the involvement of the local church Pastor-Parish Relations Committee in pastoral appointments. The ruling was that the committee's role is advisory; that consultation with the bishop and district superintendent must be done prior to the decision on the appointment; and that the parties involved are to be informed before a public announcement is made.

The process is not adhered to consistently within a given Annual Conference because not all appointments are treated in the same manner. For example, one bishop proposes giving the local church committee the right to reject or accept any proposed appointee except in the instances of the appointment of ethnic minority pastors, women pastors, or clergy couples. When it comes to these appointments, the bishop believes it is important to exercise his authority if necessary. Such a standard would undoubtedly create confusion about

DECISION MAKING

the bishop's authority and the meaning of the consultation process.

At its best, the consultation process focuses on the missional needs of a local church as these relate to the ministerial abilities of a pastor. Hence, one value of the process is that it provides an opportunity to discuss the church's mission. However, if cabinets cater primarily to the personal preferences of pastors and families, the missional purposes of The United Methodist Church may not be best served. The same may be true if cabinets give primary consideration to persuasive laypersons' preferences regarding age, sex, or race of a proposed pastor.

A second value of the consultation process is that it tends to create a better initial feeling about the appointment on the part of the pastor, the pastor's family, and the local church. This may result in short-term benefits in the early period of adjustment.

The consultative process gives more power to both pastors and congregations in appointment-making. The impression is created that the local church has authority to choose its own pastor and that the pastor can veto any proposed appointment. The result is confusion and tension about who makes decisions in pastoral appointment.

The process requires a considerable amount of the district superintendent's time. A consultation process requires a district superintendent to be involved in at least three and frequently more meetings specifically related to each appointment change. In a district with fifty to seventy or more churches and ten to twenty appointment changes per year, the time commitment is high. If the privilege of veto is given to pastors and local churches, the district superintendent and bishop become brokers of ministerial services rather than being responsible for their deployment. Thus, tension focuses on the polity definition of the tasks of both bishops and district superintendents.

The issue being highlighted is the diffusion of decision making in pastoral appointment-making. Instead of a polity which vests appointment-making in those who judge the effectiveness of clergy on the basis of ability to carry out the mission of the church, a process has been instituted which may place more emphasis on compatibility. While *The Book of Discipline* remains clear about the authority of the bishop in pastoral appointments, the practice of consultation may limit the power of the bishop and the cabinet to identify a pastor who can serve the denomination best in a particular appointment. From that point onward, the process may become negotiation rather than making the appointment and getting on with the mission of the church.

Appointment of the District Superintendent

United Methodist polity puts the appointment of district superintendents in the hands of the bishops. This procedure has survived several attempts to change it, including a reform movement of the 1820s to have presiding elders elected by the conference. Legislation to elect presiding elders failed to pass the Methodist Episcopal Church, South. Although the former Evangelical United Brethren Church elected superintendents, the practice was not incorporated into The United Methodist Church at the merger in 1968.

However, the process of appointing district superintendents is undergoing subtle change. In some parts of The United Methodist Church, bishops ask laity and clergy to suggest persons to be considered for appointment as district superintendents. Their intent is to learn the names of recognized leaders. The information is then used by the bishop in the process of appointing district superintendents.

While the authority to appoint district superintendents rests with the bishop, the process described illustrates another example of diffusion of decision making. Once it is used, the process immediately becomes more time-consuming, involves more people, and may diminish the authority of the appointment-maker. While it may be helpful for the bishop to secure names for consideration in the appointment of district superintendents, there are important implications to consider. A person who is asked for such a suggestion feels that his/her opinion will be treated seriously. Being asked to make a suggestion creates an illusion of participation. Thus, the process raises the expectation level of those consulted. Soon they feel that they have a *right* to make suggestions. The authority of the appointment-maker may be reduced somewhat when he/she hesitates to appoint other capable persons whose names did not appear on the list of suggestions.

This is not meant to denigrate the process as an unjustifiable innovation. It enables the bishop to determine which pastors are perceived as being suitable to become district superintendents. It reveals the perceived leadership ability of persons under consideration for appointment as superintendents. However, it also raises several questions: Does it tend to become a popularity contest? Does the process give a sense of participation that doesn't exist? How does it contribute to the mission of the church?

Establishing and Closing Local Churches

The discontinuation of a congregation is a pragmatic decision made on the basis of the following factors: (1) difficulty of providing pastoral leadership; (2) lack of financial resources; (3) limited missional need for the church; and (4) evidence that the remaining members are discouraged and willing to disband. This information, secured by the district superintendent, is discussed with the bishop and the cabinet. After a decision is reached the Annual Conference responds to their recommendation.

The Book of Discipline gives to the bishop and the Cabinet authority to establish new churches.[6] The local district superintendent is designated as "agent in charge." Thus, establishing a new church is an administrative decision reached by a district superintendent and later confirmed by an Annual Conference.

A complicating factor was added in 1952 requiring the district superintendent to secure approval of the site from the district Board of Church Location and Building, as well as from the district Missionary Society. In 1964 the superintendent was required to give due consideration to the home mission and church extension plans of the conference Board of Global Ministries. While these may be courtesy notifications in some instances, the required processes reduce the administrative authority once granted district superintendents by United Methodist polity. Thus, another process suggests that the missional program of the denomination is negotiable.

Programs

Practicality was the reason for the establishment of Methodism's earliest agencies. The first was in 1789, the Book Concern.[7] The founding of a publishing enterprise represented a missional concern of Methodism both to educate its people and to reach the unchurched through tracts, pamphlets, and books. The United Methodist Publishing House continues to produce the Christian education materials felt to be so important since early Methodism.

This same concern prompted John Dreisbach in 1816 to use his own money to set up a print shop for the Evangelical group. In like manner, the United Brethren in Christ established their first publishing operation in 1834. These groups were concerned that their people be literate.

In 1819 the Missionary Society was established. This was the forerunner of the current General Board of Global Ministries. In 1827 a Sunday School Union was organized. The work of this agency has become a cornerstone of the General Board of Discipleship.

During the late nineteenth and early twentieth centuries, at the time of the industrial revolution in the United States, business and government expanded their bureaucracies. Somewhat later, the denominations began their own bureaucratic expansion. Ben Primer, commenting on the Protestant Church, concludes that

> religious leaders seem to have pursued bureaucracy for its "modernity" as much as for its ability to provide coordination and control.... The Church bureaucrats sought reassurance by doing what was current.... It is

evident that they had clear doubts . . . about the effects of organization on the future of the Protestant Church. Religious leaders nevertheless overcame those doubts and sought to strengthen the Church through reorganization.[8]

The result is a group of boards and agencies that parallel business structures.

Denomination-wide emphases began as early as the Centenary Movement in 1919, an emphasis recognizing one hundred years of the Missionary Society. This was a highly organized financial campaign designed to raise funds for postwar expansion. The development of large-scale denominational programs, however, is as recent as the 1940s when existing agencies designed quadrennial programs which became precursors of denomination-wide programming. The General Conference in 1944 approved a program entitled the "Crusade for Christ" which included an emphasis on world government, raising funds to help millions of refugees created by World War II, stewardship, spirituality, and Christian education. The success of this venture encouraged the agencies to develop a program entitled "Advance for Christ and His Church" during the 1948-52 quadrennium. A result of that emphasis is the Advance program of the church which continues to solicit funds for specific mission causes and projects throughout the world.

Subsequent efforts at quadrennial programming have not been as effective. Instead, general agencies seem to vie with one another for General Conference approval of their programs. The General Conference is unwilling or incapable of focusing on a single missional emphasis. Two brief examples illustrate the dilemma.

Three missional priorities were established for the

DECISION MAKING 63

1977-80 quadrennium. Each of the major agencies was involved in some way with these concerns. New temporary structures were created for interagency consultation and decision making. Elaborate tracking charts were used to follow the progress of the programs through the various bureaucracies. Unfortunately, these programs of the agencies never gained the anticipated financial support of persons in local churches.[9]

The financial response to the Advance portion of World Hunger Missional Priority was 56 percent of the $12 million goal, or $6,737,902. The response to the Ethnic Minority Local Church Missional Priority was 8.6 percent of the $14 million goal, or $1,208,450. Throughout the qradrennium the apportioned fund for the three missional priorities ran a poor fifth among the nine apportioned funds.

Lest these figures be taken as evidence of a general lack of support for the denomination, it is noted that the response to some apportioned funds is strong. For example, the Episcopal Fund received about 99 percent, and the World Service Fund received 95 percent of their apportioned monies in 1980. However, the Black College Fund received 79.75 percent and the Ministerial Education Fund received 83 percent of its apportionments in 1980. Of over $53,222,784 apportioned in nine funds in 1980, $47,977,299 or 90 percent was paid.

The support of the apportioned funds shows strong support for the denomination and many of its programs and agencies. However, serious reservations are being raised about the apportionment system. At least three sources of such tensions are evident. A recurring tension is resistance to a "tax," as the apportionment is known by these resisters. The second area of tension is a concern that the apportionment method does not challenge people to give for missional purposes. The desire is to give people an opportunity to move beyond funding a basic budget for the denomination.

The third focus of tension, identified as "designated giving," was widely debated prior to the 1980 General Conference. The issue is: Who decides where the money goes? The proposal most widely discussed at the 1980 General Conference would have encouraged members to select among the various general funds those which they would support. They would be encouraged to give an amount which would be equal to the total of the apportionment assigned to the congregation.

Varying levels of support for general church funds indicate that local churches are exercising designation in their giving. At the same time, some are asking, "What do our apportionments produce?" One clergy member of an annual conference Council on Finance and Administration expressed his feelings in these words, "The Annual Conference and the general church are parasites on the local church." Evidently the priorities of the general church and Annual Conference are not always the priorities of the local church. Continued support of Annual Conference and general church structures cannot be taken for granted simply because the support has been given in the past.

For the 1981-84 quadrennium, the General Conference established only one missional priority, but it also adopted five special programs. In effect, the number of major emphases increased from three to six. The general agencies in fact agreed to participate in a single missional priority as long as each could develop its own special program.

The current situation is that the general agencies, established because of particular needs at particular times, have expanded into formidable bureaucracies. As with all bureaucratic structures, the general agencies feel it necessary to justify their existence and protect their turf. Therefore, they have assumed responsibility to provide the denomination with programs in their areas of concern. The General Conference, composed in part of persons who hold memberships on the general agencies, has not been able to provide the denomination with a single missional emphasis which unifies the denomination.

Conferences

The conferences of United Methodism are the backbone of polity. These bodies make decisions affecting every United Methodist church and every member. However, because of time pressure and volume of business, conference decisions frequently are made following very little discussion by the full body. Conferences do not create proposals, but respond to those created by groups in the conferences or the denomination. As a result, the Annual Conferences are perceived as bodies which ratify or legitimize decisions by others.

The General Conference is the denomination-wide governing body. Its legislation forms the polity of the church. In this respect, its decisions affect every local church and, to some extent, every United Methodist. Only it can authorize changes in *The Book of Discipline*.

The General Conference is composed of delegates elected by Annual Conferences. Annual Conference elections produce two groups of delegates. One group is composed of lay and clergy who are recognized for their leadership. They are chosen because they can represent the interests and needs of the conference. Members of the other group are chosen because of their Annual Conference leadership in and representation of special interest groups such as ethnic minorities, young persons, and women in ministry. The result is that the composition of General Conference encourages a politicized arena for special interest groups.

All General Conference delegates serve as members of standing legislative committees dealing with petitions, resolutions, or other matters assigned to them. The choices for membership assignments to the standing legislative committees are made by the delegates themselves within the Annual Conference delegations.

Petitions, containing proposed changes in *The Book of Discipline,* are submitted by general agencies, annual conference local churches, and individuals. The immensity of the delegates' task is illustrated by the more than twenty thousand petitions representing over five thousand different matters to be considered in one week at the 1980 General Conference. It would have taken ninety-seven working hours for a legislative committee to give only five minutes to each separate title referred to it. Because attention cannot be given to that many petitions, legislative subcommittees are formed to review each petition. Even so, some petitions receive only passing attention.

The losers are petitions from local churches and individuals. Since many of them are unique, they are

DECISION MAKING 67

dismissed following a quick review. Petitions from agencies, on the other hand, receive more attention and influence the denomination. There are several reasons for this.

First, the general agencies have their petitions printed in pre-conference reports which delegates receive before they go to the General Conference. Thus, delegates have an opportunity to consider these petitions before experiencing the pressures of the conference. Furthermore, the more important proposals are discussed in the church press before the opening of General Conference.

Second, in addition to appearing in pre-conference reports, general agency petitions have had careful review and refinement before being submitted. They are prepared by staff and then are reviewed and refined by the voting members of the general agencies. Since the voting members of the general agencies are members of Annual Conferences, the petitions receive widespread attention and discussion.

Third, many members of the agencies are elected as delegates to General Conference. It is not uncommon for such a delegate to choose to serve in the legislative committee which considers the concerns for the agency of which he/she is a member. This delegate and general agency member then becomes an advocate and interpreter of the proposed legislation.

Due to the delegate selection process and the weight given to agency petitions, all petitions do not receive equal attention. Persons supporting and interpreting legislation in which they have a personal interest or investment exert a substantial influence in General Conference *even when the specific piece of legislation involved has not been reviewed from the perspective of the mission of the total denomination.* In this respect General Conference includes both special interest groups and people who have a special stake in the continued existence of the denomination's bureaucracy.

The presence of general agency staff at General Conference also influences decision making. They often serve as resource persons for legislative committees and as advisors for the delegates. These persons *are not staff of the General Conference* but of the agencies which are proposing legislation and seeking financial support for the next quadrennium.

Undue influence of the general agencies at General Conference may well have contributed to hostility found among pastors and local churches toward general agencies and their programs. Thus, tension and frustration have been generated by the issues of appropriate role and balance of influence at General Conference.

Annual Conferences, "the basic body of the Church," probably should have a stronger voice in General Conference. The tension at this point is similar to that between national and state levels of government. For example, the Annual Conference appears to be caught between the General Conference and the local church.[10] General Conference establishes policies in pensions, ministerial standards, apportionments, and programs which require Annual Conference implementation. Local church resistance to these is directed toward the Annual Conference, along with feelings aroused by pastoral changes, apportionments, and programs.

United Methodist polity historically has tended to represent experiences from local congregations and has sought to provide service to local congregations. If The United Methodist Church is to be a serious force for the gospel, it must establish conferences which, in membership, represent the entire church. Furthermore, it must give serious consideration to all legislative proposals rather than believing that all worthwhile legislation must be generated by or come through agencies.

Finally, the conferences must provide opportunity for inspiration, celebration, and worship for large gatherings of United Methodists. Recharging the spirits of clergy and laity is as important a function for an Annual or General Conference as working in legislative committees. The church should be experienced as the church in conference settings as well as in local church gatherings. United Methodists gathered to make decisions in conferences need to have their spirits fed. The spark which comes from the inspiration of larger groups can inspire and empower the church.

Funding

It takes money to support local churches, district superintendents, bishops, conferences, and general agencies of the church. As a consequence funding decisions are very important at all levels of the church.

During the past decade some shifts have occurred in the distribution of money by the local church, the major funding source for the entire connection. Besides exercising selectivity in allocating funds to the general church, local churches are spending more for their own operating expenses and ministerial support. *The number one priority of local churches during the 1970s was the care of pastors.*[11] While the increasing costs of pension programs and health benefit programs were major factors in the shift, the *significant factor* is that local churches and

Annual Conferences decided this was their priority, not the general church which had other priorities!

A smaller proportion of the local church dollar went to connectional funds and benevolences in 1979 than in 1970. If local churches had allocated their 1979 money as they did in 1970, about $20 *million* more annually would have been available for connectional and benevolent purposes. This would have translated into $5 *million* more for World Service and Conference Benevolences.

The apportionment system, used for years in the antecedent groups of The United Methodist Church, has produced commendable results as noted earlier. However, response to various funds has not been uniform. Apportionments are not as binding on local churches as are the appointment of a pastor and the property trust clause. The 1980 General Conference changed the local church method of approving apportionments. Now local churches are notified by a conference official of the amount to be paid by that church for World Service and Conference Benevolences. Although there are no sanctions to ensure collection, some local churches saw the action as the demise of another local decision-making option in favor of centralized control.

Although the apportionment system historically was received positively, it has been experienced often as a tax or franchise fee. It is looked on by some as debt paying rather than participation in mission. It does not create joy and enthusiasm among the givers. Yet the system is clear in its expectations, equitable in its distribution, and has a history of successful use.

The perception of many local churches is that they exist to provide money for the Annual Conference and the general church where the *real* mission is conducted. Such a reversal of original polity causes frustration in local churches. Payment of apportionments is even a measure of the success or failure of a local church pastor, thus strengthening the local church's impression that it is being used as a funding tool for denominational levels beyond it.

The apportionment system works well in a denomination where there is a common mission, a relationship of trust among the levels of the system, and effective dissemination of information.

The positive response to the Advance program, when viewed alongside the widespread unease with the apportionment system, suggests the need to explore possible supplements to apportionments as means to fund the denomination. One survey indicates that United Methodists give: (1) to help meet human need, (2) to win persons to Christ, and (3) to express gratitude to God.[12] These motives support the mission purpose on which Methodist polity was originally built.

Our polity provides for funding decisions to be made at levels where local church funds are received and distributed. One of these centers is the annual conference Council on Finance and Administration (CFA). In recent years the CFA has begun consulting with the Council on Ministries on programmatic matters. Even so, the CFA controls budget maximums by setting budget limits and making final budget recommendations to the Annual Conference.

When we consider the funding of general agencies, we become aware of the fact that the key to agencies is their money. They exist as long as they can justify their need for funds. Agency leaders know it is important to increase budget requests continually and to spend the current monies in full. If the general agency did not spend all its money, it would be open to the charge of not needing its money and would be in danger of having it reduced in the coming year.

Some United Methodists who have been taught to work hard, spend sparingly, give generously, and save, find it difficult to justify continued support of general agencies when local needs are so great. On the other hand, agencies are in business not to make a profit or to save, but to spend. They spend on staff, travel, buildings, and, decreasingly over the past few years, on program.

In the resolution of funding issues, there must be a feeling of partnership in the connection. Tensions caused by funding can be detrimental to any organization. In its effort to channel its tensions creatively perhaps The United Methodist Church will review general agency structures to determine their most appropriate form and functions to support the mission of the church in its third century.

Congregations

The local church is one of the most important points of decision in The United Methodist Church. While budgets may be set and programs may be adopted at higher levels in the connection, the final decision to support them is made by the local church. When local congregations are willing to implement decisions made by General or Annual Conferences, the system appears to be hierarchical; that is, it appears that everything falls into line with what has happened at higher levels. On the other hand, when a congregation rejects or ignores a decision made at another level of the system, it becomes clear that compliance with decisions made elsewhere in the system is based on voluntary cooperation by the local church.

The Charge Conference is the body where the local church and the connection meet. Decisions reserved for the Charge Conference are: (1) removal of persons from the membership roll of the local church, (2) recommendation of persons considered to be suitable candidates for ministry, (3) election of local church officers and members of boards and committees, (4) setting the salary and other remuneration for the pastor, (5) receiving reports, reviewing and evaluating the total mission of the church, and (6) adopting objectives and goals for the church.[13]

While most decisions of the Charge Conference are ratifications, it is the primary connectional experience for a local church. This meeting with a connectional representative provides an opportunity for the objectives of the total denomination to be interpreted and allows opportunities for questions to be raised and issues to be discussed with the district superintendent. It also gives the district superintendents firsthand experience with the local church program and a chance to observe the pastor's leadership style.

One measure of the health of an organization is the degree of compliance with its policies and actions. On this basis The United Methodist Church scores well. Major tensions in the denomination revolve around the influence the general agencies have on General Conference, and the decisions they make about program and other matters.

It is important to remember that compliance of individual members and local churches in United

Methodism is voluntary. For example, the decision to begin a new church is made by the district superintendent, the cabinet, and the conference. Yet if laypersons who are close to the site of the new church do not support it by attending, participating in programs, and giving their money, decisions made by others are meaningless.

In almost every instance, starting a new church requires the cooperation of pastors and members of existing United Methodist churches. They help identify, perhaps train, and support the beginning cadre of workers and worshipers who will become the new church. In addition, the existing churches often help some people decide to join the new venture. None of these decisions is mandatory; they are all voluntary.

Thus, it is a fact of our polity that in decision making the denomination relies on voluntary compliance of local units. With the exception of the trust clause, most decisions made beyond the local church have no binding obligation. On the other hand, decisions made elsewhere provide many opportunities for supplying resources, counsel, and financial assistance for the local church. Those other decisions also provide a means for a local church to become a partner in the mission enterprises of The United Methodist Church around the world. Facilities and personnel for training clergy are a result of those decisions as well. It thus becomes apparent that the system is an interlocking one whose components are mutually dependent.

This chapter has identified tensions that revolve around decision making. Areas of tension include sharing decisions in pastoral appointment-making, the method for selecting district superintendents, establishing and closing churches, role of general agencies in

DECISION MAKING

General Conference and program development, role and functions of various conferences in United Methodism, funding decisions, and congregations. These tensions are generated by an unclear perception of roles of laypersons, district superintendents, bishops, general agencies, conferences, and congregations. Furthermore, although The United Methodist Church looks like a hierarchical system, its decision making is diffused, and implementation of its decisions depends on voluntary compliance.

Our next task is to look at tensions within the context of leadership.

CHAPTER 4

Leadership

Those who set directions for others to follow are leaders. Leaders of The United Methodist Church set directions for the denomination. When asked, "Who do you see leading The United Methodist Church today?" both clergy and laity responded, "I don't see (anyone) anywhere." While this may be accurate with regard to one type of leadership, United Methodism is not leaderless.

There are two types of leadership, symbolic and functional.[1] Symbolic leadership has a role and accompanying role expectations (e.g., pastors). Functional or operational leadership plans and executes programs.

United Methodism does not have one or two symbolic spokespersons who can unify or speak for the denomination. On the other hand, the denomination can and does initiate, develop, and implement programs through countless leaders at the general, annual conference, district, and congregational levels. These are functional leaders.

The term "leader" usually refers to an individual. United Methodist polity has been designed so that leadership is not in the hands of individuals, but of groups. At the general church level these groups include the Council of Bishops, General Council on Ministries, General Council on Finance and Administration, and other agencies. While most agencies have staff who exert much influence, no person is or would be authorized to be *the* leader for the entire United Methodist denomination.

Tensions within The United Methodist Church in the area of leadership center around changing roles of bishops and general agencies, as well as ambivalence about the desirability of strong leadership. Tension is also focused on clergy domination of the church. In this chapter we will explore a model of leadership and explore where the model might be placed most effectively.

Leadership in United Methodism

The 1972-76 Quadrennial Commission for the Study of the Offices of Bishops and District Superintendents reported that one of the paradoxical revelations of their research is the "suspicion of leadership joined with the cry for leadership."[2] The Commission suggested that the denomination acknowledge "the need for leadership and . . . find ways to set leaders free and to support them in their leadership roles."[3]

This ambivalence toward strong leadership harasses United Methodism. Leadership is strongly desired. However, members of an Annual Conference planning retreat in 1980 agreed that if individuals begin to lead, their peers find ways to "cut the leaders off at the knees" so they can no longer stand out. This illustration could apply to most conferences and agencies in United Methodism. Leadership is desired but feared. These twin poles have existed in United Methodist polity from the beginning.

While leadership is being feared, it is being assumed

and used by various groups and agencies within the church. Ethnic minority caucuses and special interest groups have surfaced to lead particular groups for specific causes. Leaders of these caucuses had no intention of being leaders for the denomination. Their aim was to make the denomination responsive to their needs and desires. They have become functional leaders in a narrow sphere. They continue to exist because they have found supportive groups which follow their lead.

Bishops are seen by local church pastors and laypersons as the visible leaders of the church. While their role has changed substantially over the years, bishops for most United Methodists serve a symbolic role quite effectively.[4]

Laypersons are assuming more leadership roles. Their insistence on sharing power has resulted in adaptations of the pastoral appointment process. In addition, they have demanded and received more opportunities for participation in the powerful councils of the church. The Lay Address to the 1980 General Conference was virtually an announcement of laity's continuing demand for more leadership opportunities.

United Methodism is not without leadership. It simply has a problem in allowing leaders to be legitimated. It has an additional problem of allowing leaders to function as leaders. To complicate these problems, it accepts leadership from a variety of sources, none of which has the total denomination in mind.

Leadership in the Past

One reason United Methodism has a divided opinion about leadership stems from its beginnings. John

Wesley, leader of the Methodist societies in England, was acknowledged by members and preachers as their leader. His leadership made the future of the denomination possible. He assigned preachers, created the conference structure for England, ordained and assigned leaders for America, and developed the outdoor evangelistic preaching that made Methodism a power in England.

Immigrants brought the Methodist movement to the American colonies. Local Methodist preachers became functional leaders among the immigrants, and were the "troops" which firmly established the Methodist movement in the New World. Wesley, responding to their pleas, sent itinerant preachers to work with the new societies, but seven of the eight returned to England when the American Revolution began.

America has been the land of freedom in many ways. The desire of American Methodists to be free, while continuing to reflect the ties to Wesley, created tensions. "One important element in American Methodist progress during the 1770s was the struggle for power between the pioneer local preachers and their absent leader, operating through ... itinerant preachers dispatched with delegated authority to guide the fortunes of the new societies."[5]

In 1771, Francis Asbury was sent to America to put the Methodists in order. In 1772, after he had established a sixteen-point reform plan, Asbury became Wesley's assistant in charge of all American work.[6] Between 1773 and 1778, however, Thomas Rankin was the assistant. Only after 1778 was Asbury given power and authority to shape American Methodism.

Asbury established the climate which made possible the formation of the Methodist Episcopal Church. He felt that preachers should decide on the formation and polity of the new denomination. He insisted on a General Conference to approve the new constitution and the ordination of Coke and himself as general superintendents. He was the leader.

The leadership pattern for the Evangelical Association and the United Brethren differed only in style. Since these were regional movements, the leaders were founders or persons influential in local settings. Albright was elected a bishop of the Evangelical Association in 1807 but died in 1808. Their next bishop was elected in 1839.

Otterbein and Boehm were designated "elders" at the United Brethren Conference of 1800. The term "bishop" was not used until 1813. Other early influential leaders were Christian Newcomer for the United Brethren and John Dreisbach in the Evangelical Association.

While these persons were important in each of the strands of United Methodism, the real power rested in the conferences. The deliberative body was more to be trusted than an individual. It was in the Annual Conference that issues were discussed, planning occurred, and pastors were appointed. Leadership at these conferences was by designation or election and by those preachers who, by charisma or reputation, created followers.

The Bishops as Leaders

During the first sixteen years of the Methodist Episcopal Church, the office of bishop became a key leadership position, especially under the direction of Asbury. Early bishops traveled across the entire

LEADERSHIP

connection and were well-known figures. They were leaders of the total denomination.

The office of the general superintendent or bishop in the Methodist Church at the close of the eighteenth century was a powerful one.

1. He was elected by and responsible to General Conference.
2. He considered himself to be consecrated as a bishop, implying something different from the apostolic episcopacy, but representing a different office from that of elder.
3. There was an acceptance of his role as educator of the clergy and editor of the publications of the church.
4. He was responsible for the appointment of pastors.
5. His appointments were not subject to review by presiding elders or clergy.
6. He had the rights of ordination of deacons and elders, and consecration of other bishops.
7. He could exercise veto power in the matter of ordination.
8. He was required to travel "throughout the connection." (The failure of Coke to do this eventually led to his resignation.)
9. He was empowered to establish special ministries, such as the power to ordain Negro deacons.
10. He presided over sessions of Annual and General Conference.
11. He designated presiding elders and determined their term of office within the limits established by General Conference.
12. He was morally subject to General Conference, which had established procedures for the trial of bishops.

13. He was the supreme law officer and could act as an appellate court on matters of denominational law.
14. He could prevent a preacher from publishing or circulating literature antagonistic to the church.[7]

While some of these functions changed through the years, the office of bishop continued to be important. In the union of 1939, the newly formed Methodist Church gave the Council of Bishops responsibility "to plan for the general oversight and promotion of the temporal and spiritual interests of the entire church."[8] A similar assignment was given to the bishops in 1968 when The United Methodist Church was formed.

Fear of the bishop's power has been a part of our denominational experience. This is one reason for the thirty-one-year period between the first two bishops of the Evangelical Association. The delay was ascribed to "the fear that the office of bishop would accumulate inordinate power."[9] Because of this fear General Conference has taken some actions to limit the bishop's authority.

Currently bishops are elected for life, although attempts have been made to limit a bishop's service to a fixed term. While this was the original plan in the United Brethren Church, it was changed to a life term by 1826. The 1972-76 Study Commission concluded that "most of the reasons for term episcopacy dealt with the personal misuse of power rather than with the office as such."[10]

The Changing Role of the Bishop

The earliest General Conference included bishops and all preachers serving Methodist societies. As the denomination grew, it became increasingly difficult for all preachers to attend the conference. In 1808 the General Conference of the Methodist Episcopal Church approved representative membership for succeeding General Conferences. A plan for selecting delegates was established. Bishops were given responsibilities as presiding officers but were disqualified from participating in legislative functions.

The Methodist Episcopal Church was very concerned about the power of bishops. In 1884 it adopted a rule allowing bishops to speak in General Conference sessions only if permission was granted by the body. Another rule held that a bishop could not close debate on an issue even though he had chaired the committee.

Other actions by the northern church which limited the office of bishop were the appointment of missionary bishops to function in specific geographic areas and the assignment of bishops to episcopal areas. Thus, the bishop was effectively limited to a geographical area in which he functioned as president of Annual Conference(s).

When The Methodist Church was formed in 1939, bishops lost the right to determine the number of districts in an Annual Conference. The simultaneous formation of the Judicial Council removed from the bishop the power of final judicial decisions. Establishment of the jurisdiction structure of the denomination resulted in later changes for the bishop.

More recent changes in The United Methodist Church include the formation of the Jurisdictional Committee on Nominations as well as limits on the number of years a bishop may be assigned to an episcopal area. One commentator said, "On this point the roles of bishops and pastors have been exactly reversed: the early bishops had no limits on either their tenure or their scope of activity, but the preachers had to move every year. The current bishops are limited in tenure and in scope of service, whereas there are no limits on tenure of pastors."[11]

Murray H. Leiffer identified several changes in the authority of bishops in The Methodist Church between 1940 and 1960. Among these were (1) quadrennial emphases, which took from the bishop responsibility for program making, and (2) the requirement of consultation with the cabinet in appointment-making.[12] Frederick Norwood, commenting on the same period, notes the primary reason for the changes. "A force of increasing influence was the collective power of the administrative secretaries of the national boards and commissions. The bishops became aware—unhappily—that much of the leadership in developing quadrennial programs rested in the hands of the Council of Secretaries and the Coordinating Council."[13]

As a result of these changes bishops have become more and more limited to symbolic leadership, while functional leadership has been assigned to more and more groups. As Norwood indicated earlier, some of the more influential of those groups are the general agencies.

The Role of General Agencies

In 1942 the Council of Bishops of The Methodist Church convened the members of the Commission on World Service and Finance, the Executive Committee of the Woman's Division of Christian Service, and the Council of Secretaries to reflect on Methodism's part in the world situation.[14] Out of that meeting came the quadrennial emphasis, Crusade for Christ, followed by a second quadrennial program, both of which were very successful.

These successes led the 1952 General Conference to legislate quadrennial programming. The Coordinating Council (a representative group of lay and clergy persons at the national level) was to develop these programs in consultation with the Council of Bishops and the Council of Secretaries. Even though the Council of Bishops continued to provide suggestions, they lost their direct programming power through this shift of polity. In their stead, the staff of the general agencies collectively became more important in program development.[15]

The two major reasons for this shift appear to be (1) Methodism's historic fear of the power of the episcopacy and (2) cultural adaptation by the general agencies of the bureaucratic model since 1940. The rise of general agencies coincided with a feeling that bureaucracy was effective in getting things done. Thus, functional leadership powers of bishops were whittled away.

The dangers of this shift of functional leadership have not been fully appreciated. In the first place, agencies have no constitutional authority. They are creatures whose authority is defined by General Conference. The fact that structures can be changed without constitutional amendment is an expression of United Methodism's flexibility and practicality. There is, however, no system of checks and balances to define the authority of general agencies as there is for conference, the episcopacy, and the judiciary.

Because of the great influence general agencies have

on General Conference, they have an opportunity to define their own responsibilities. On the other hand, without constitutional authority, general agencies have no guaranteed existence.

A second danger is more potent. Bureaucratic structures allow opportunities for general agency staff to meet regularly for interaction, planning, evaluation, and implementation. This is a proper and necessary set of functions. As a result of such opportunities, these groups gain much more influence and cohesion than those staffed by volunteers, whose endeavors are not nurtured by regular and extended association. In short, the staff of agencies are full time, while bishops and elected members give only part-time attention to programming.

A third danger is that since the denomination has no designated chief executive officer, each agency functions independently. This produces competition and tension. The General Council on Ministries and the General Council on Finance and Administration offer some limited coordination which is subject to review by General Conference.

The upshot is that the staff of general agencies can and do use their resources to develop "game plans" to achieve their own ends. No other body in the church has such leadership resources available to influence the direction of the denomination.

A Leadership Model for the Church

A leadership model for the church requires careful review and adjustment of the roles of the Council of Bishops and general agencies. It must establish a system of checks and balances for the agencies comparable to the other aspects of the polity. Connectionalism in United Methodism relies on clearly defined and shared authority. A leadership model for the church must function with these twin realities.

In a perceptive discussion of "Transforming Leadership," James M. Burns suggests five characteristics which might be useful for The United Methodist Church to consider.[16]

1. *Transforming leadership is collective.* One-person leadership is a contradiction in terms. There must be continuing interaction between leader and followers not only to "collect" information to assist in the development of goals and values, but also to "coalesce" the faithful into an effective working body. Interaction produces changes in both the leader's and the follower's motives and goals.

2. *Transforming leadership is dissensual.* Effective leadership is not afraid of conflict, but encourages or even initiates it around key issues. In contrast, the consensual type of leadership is paralyzed until there is a supposed unity or agreement. In today's church there is a growing desire for leaders to take initiatives.

3. *Transforming leadership is causative.* The causative leader makes things happen. In the church this means things happen only after appropriate interaction has taken place between leaders and followers—actions which are in keeping with its values.

4. *Transforming leadership is morally purposeful.* Effective leadership points in a direction and helps choose values and goals. Burns says, "Both leaders and followers are drawn into the shaping of purpose . . . the transforming leader taps the needs and raises the

aspirations and helps to shape the values—and hence mobilizes the potential—of followers."[17]

5. *Transforming leadership is elevating.* Leadership asks for sacrifice from followers rather than promising them desired results. As a consequence, "both leaders and followers are raised to more principled levels of judgment."[18]

The question raised is Where should The United Methodist Church legitimate this kind of leadership? Leadership exists in United Methodism, and leaders are followed. Unfortunately, leaders and followers are *segmented* into special interests and groups, rather than being *connected* through a single desire or purpose. Where United Methodists look for that unifying leadership will make the difference in the future of the denomination.

In considering the leadership model it is helpful to examine possible consequences of locating the leadership in specific groups.

1. *General Agencies of the Church*

The general agencies of the church cannot and should not fulfill this type of leadership. There is widespread distrust of the agencies by pastors and laity alike. Agencies are considered to be far removed from the local congregation, unwilling to respond to correspondence, addressing themselves to clientele other than the local church, creating problems because of controversial stands on social issues, and conducting unnecessary and overlapping functions. For many United Methodists, the general agencies represent "the other church."

General agencies by definition and assignment deal with different and specific areas of responsibility.

LEADERSHIP

General Conference has continually attempted to focus the work of the agencies by creating a structure for coordination. The Council of Secretaries (1940) in The Methodist Church, The Council of Administration (1946) in the Evangelical United Brethren Church, the Coordinating Council (1952) of The Methodist Church, the Program Council (1968), and the General Council on Ministries (1972) of The United Methodist Church, all have been efforts to focus the resources of the general agencies of the church.

In addition to these external efforts at coordination, internal efforts are being made. Evaluation and goal setting within the agencies have resulted partly from work of the General Council on Ministries.[19] The full effect of these on the life of the agencies, as they relate to the mission of the church, has yet to be seen. While these efforts are commendable, the fact remains that each agency shares in only one phase of the mission activity of the church, thus limiting its ability to lead.

Finally, the general agencies cannot lead because there is no consensus about the mission of the denomination. If such a consensus did exist, the general agencies would still be left to their own devices to initiate and develop programs they felt would benefit the church. The unfortunate fact is that General Conference approves these programs without a consensus about the church's mission.

In the 1940s it became time to create denomination-wide special emphases. The programs were important and effective. The tensions described in this book suggest that it may be time for the creation of a different type of response for the future. Energies and resources of the denomination *must* be focused, probably in the direction of the local church. Key leadership, therefore, must be given by those who are in touch with the local church.

2. *Council of Bishops*

Several characteristics of the Council of Bishops place it in a unique position to give leadership to the church. First, the Council represents a continuity of experience. At the November, 1981, meeting, a bishop was present who had been elected in 1944. This means the Council had available a person with thirty-seven years of a bishop's leadership experience on which to draw. Two of the bishops elected in 1980 may serve for twenty years as active bishops. With existing tenure limitation rules in the church, no other body can have that degree of continuity.

Bishops are elected. The process of becoming a bishop is complex, but it does require peer approval and election. No other leadership position in the denomination has such a requirement.

The Council of Bishops is in touch with all sections of the church. The regional differences can be dealt with by the Council since bishops there know these differences well. Cultural problems are real in the church, but a group who is in touch with the variety of cultural forces in the regions can deal with them effectively.

The suggestion of the 1964 report of "The Study of the General Superintendency of The Methodist Church" remains applicable. It stated, "It is suggested that the Council of Bishops should accept a broader responsibility for leadership in the church as a whole." The Council should take initiative to identify needs, and then take necessary steps to use the resources of the denomination to deal with these needs.

Only if two conditions are met can the Council of Bishops give the leadership needed. The first is the need for a full-time person designated by the Council to give leadership and guidance to its life and work. In 1968 General Conference endorsed a proposal that one bishop be elected to serve as full-time secretary for the Council. The proposal died because it did not receive approval by two-thirds of the Annual Conferences. After revision to assure proper checks and balances so as not to allow too much power in one individual's hands, the concept of the plan needs to be revived, discussed, and endorsed by the church.

The second condition for effective leadership by bishops is to have a resident bishop in each Annual Conference. Only when a bishop's energies and attention are focused on a single conference can he or she provide the symbolic *and* functional leadership required in the complex social settings of current and future times.

A final issue deals with the election process of bishops. Social organizations, including the church, generally elect the type of leaders they want. However, most other social organizations do not elect their leaders for life. Nomination by an Annual Conference for episcopal election reflects admirable performance in the Annual Conference. It does not necessarily mean that the nominee is capable or qualified to be a general superintendent. If a bishop does not perform well in the position, there is no process readily available to replace that person prior to retirement. The needed system, designed to surface the most capable leaders, must make clear both what the leader will be expected to do and what the leader will be permitted to do.

3. *The Role of the Clergy*

"... *ALL* the early beginnings, including Virginia and Pennsylvania as well as New York, were by laymen, generally operating under the designation of 'local preacher.' Of course, they were not ordained. They were not even under the regular appointment as traveling preacher. What they did, they did on their own initiative, or that of their friends who urged them on. The planting of Methodism in America was a lay movement."[20] Many women, too, were involved from the beginning; Barbara Heck, an Irish immigrant to New York, serves as a symbol of the significant influence of laywomen in the church.

While it began as a lay movement, it became quickly a clergy church. Annual Conferences, for the first century of the denomination's life, were composed solely of ordained itinerant preachers. In spite of this, laity led local congregations. Since pastors served a circuit of churches, they left the day-to-day care and operation of the church to laity. The pastors' roles were to preach, administer the sacraments, provide for nurture, and enforce the discipline of the church.

As pastors began to settle down in the early nineteenth century, they assumed more functions in the daily life of congregations, such as nominating laypersons for leadership. In 1884 the Methodist Episcopal *Discipline* listed more than one hundred duties assigned to the pastor.

Under the itinerant clergy system, the class meeting had provided "the sub-pastoral oversight made necessary by our itinerant economy."[21] The class leader was a necessary adjunct to the pastor. With the settling of the clergy, however, the class meeting became unnecessary. Thus, Norwood observes, "Inadvertently, because of the settling down of the traveling preacher, Methodism lost one of its strongest supports, the active *ministerial* participation of the lay people."[22]

Laity were not displaced without a struggle. Out of the reform struggles of the first quarter of the nineteenth century came the Methodist Episcopal Church, which provided for equal representation of clergy and laity in its General Conference of 1830. In 1870, the Methodist Episcopal Church, South, took this step; in 1876 the Methodist Episcopal Church provided for two lay delegates from each Annual Conference. The United Brethren Church had equal lay and clergy representation in General Conference by 1888, as did the Evangelical Association by 1903. Equal representation was not achieved in the Methodist Episcopal Church until 1932.

It also took a struggle for women delegates to be admitted to General Conference. In 1888, five women who had been elected as delegates to the Methodist Episcopal Church General Conference were not permitted to be seated. In 1896 four women were seated, and in 1900 women's equality was approved in the new constitution. The Methodist Protestant Church had admitted women as delegates in 1892; the Methodist Episcopal Church, South, approved women delegates in 1922.

Recent legislative changes have provided additional lay involvement and have done even more to curtail clergy domination. In 1939 pastors in The Methodist Church were no longer required to chair the Official Board of the local church. Although the position of lay leader was established, the role is not clear.

Laypersons outnumber clergy as members of many general and Annual Conference agencies. Laypersons serve on Committees on Episcopacy and District Committees on Superintendency, where they counsel bishops and district superintendents about their work. The local church Committee on Pastor-Parish Relations, which is now reponsible for evaluating pastors, is comprised solely of laypersons.

These changes have placed laity in positions of power and decision making. They make it possible for laity to have a larger part in the kinds of symbolic and functional leadership previously reserved for clergy.

A Concluding Reminder

While The United Methodist Church has provided for more significant involvement of laypersons in the life of the church, it has not developed a modern counterpart to the kind of missional lay involvement typified by the class meeting of an earlier era. Lay leadership at the local church must be encouraged and enabled in this kind of discipleship for laypersons need to be more than policymakers in the church.

The model of leadership outlined in this chapter needs to be discussed widely throughout the denomination. We must come to a renewed understanding of the role of the bishops as key leaders, of the general agencies as resourcing bodies, and of the laypersons as active participants in the mission of the total church.

As United Methodists we must come again to a clear understanding of our principle tasks and mission in the name of Christ. The leadership of the denomination must provide guidance and direction for this. As United Methodists we must again actively live out this mission in our lives. The leaders must set the example for us all. As

LEADERSHIP

United Methodists we must motivate the laypersons and ministers alike to devote their energies to this mission. And our leaders must come forward to provide the inspiration and the wisdom to focus our talents to accomplish the task. Our denomination has often held ambivalent feelings regarding strong leadership. Notwithstanding, the need is present for persons with vision and courage to state the mission, to show the direction, to set the example, and to lead.

CHAPTER 5

Evaluation

Modern-day organizations are characterized by an insistence on evaluation, whether relating to personnel performance, program effectiveness, or organizational concerns. Within the past ten years, evaluation has become an established and expected process. It is done with varying levels of effectiveness.

In recent years formal evaluation has become a part of the polity of The United Methodist Church. In this chapter we will review evaluation provisions, and consider the tensions surrounding the implementation of evaluation.

An important factor in effective evaluation is the establishment of measurable criteria which carry the authority of either official action or mutual consent of the evaluator(s) and those being evaluated.

One difficulty of evaluation in the church comes at the point of measurable criteria. For example, persons being examined for admission into full connection or associate membership in an Annual Conference are asked the historical question, "Are you going on to perfection?" While this is obviously an expectation, it is not a measurable criterion.

Lay leaders of local churches who experience evaluation in their work wish to establish such a process in the local church. Sometimes they are inclined to use as the basis for evaluating ministerial performance easily measurable criteria such as the number of new members received, worship attendance, and the number of pastoral calls made. While these are measurable, they may not measure ministerial performance effectively. Other, less tangible factors are just as critical. These include spiritual growth of members, their willingness to become involved in ministries within and beyond the local church, and other matters relating to the spiritual climate of a local church.[1]

Evaluation in United Methodism

Only recently has evaluation become an organizational process in The United Methodist Church. For example, since 1968 the annual Charge Conference has been required to evaluate the ministry of the local church.[2] In 1976 the General Council on Ministries was charged "to review and evaluate the effectiveness of the general program agencies in performing the ministries assigned to them."[3] Their evaluations, to be reported to the General Conference, are to contain recommendations for continuance or discontinuance of general agency programs.

Evaluation of bishops, district superintendents, and pastors was legislated in the 1976 General Conference. Committees are to consult with these leaders and appraise their performance.

Thus, in recent years the emphasis of evaluation has been on leadership, the effectiveness of local churches, and the work of general agencies. This represents a major shift in the historic evaluation pattern of United Methodism. In early Methodism, evaluation was focused on the local church member. Local church members in those early societies were expected to live according to the precepts of the gospel as these were interpreted by the societies. To ignore or fail to carry out the expectations could lead to expulsion. Will future directions of the connection build on or reject the past? A review of the concept of evaluation in United Methodism may help us explore directions.

The "Bottom Line"

"The bottom line is what counts" is a statement heard often in business and industry. To corporations the "bottom line" means the amount of profit left after accounting for all income and subtracting all expenses. What remains may be distributed to shareholders or used to help a corporation pursue its objectives.

For the church, the "bottom line" has a different connotation. In original Methodist polity, regardless of the branch, the "bottom line" was mission to individuals. The mission was a very pragmatic process of winning souls to Christ, gathering them into classes for instruction, offering mutual support and discipline, and establishing a procedure for caring for one another. The only condition for membership in these societies was "a desire to flee from the wrath to come." The societies were characterized by a devotional spirit, high moral standards, and programs of social service. These agenda were established by Wesley when society members were presumed to be members of the Church of England.

Because Methodism was viewed as a missionary movement, the early societies in America reflected the same "bottom line." For Asbury, the essential matter was "living to God." This meant that every Methodist was expected to have a conversion experience, remain spiritually alive, and maintain high standards of morality, stewardship, and discipline.[4]

Methodist conferences were organized to enable and ensure that the desired results were attained. Wesley created the connection of preachers to achieve the missional goal. The conferences were to teach the doctrine, discipline the preachers, and review their practice. The Annual Conference was where the results of local efforts could be reported, the goals of the movement renewed, and the preachers inspired.

In early Methodism there were no General Conference requirements for general agencies.[5] Instead, pastors were responsible to see that people were won to Christ and that their lives were changed as they moved on to perfection. Later, the church established agencies to support pastors and laypersons in achieving these purposes. For example, the general Board of Missions was created to establish new churches through which people might be won and nurtured in the faith. The publishing enterprise had the same two functions, winning the lost and nurturing the faithful. The Chartered Fund was to care for the preachers (whose task was to win and nurture) and their widows. The early ventures in education were in evangelism and nurture.[6]

Changes in the Focus of Evaluation

On the way to the twenty-first century, society put some cultural pressures on United Methodists, and the "bottom line" changed. The desire of laity to be heard resulted in a split in American Methodism during its first half century. A Civil War resulted in the division of the church. The revivals of the early 1800s brought with them the uniqueness of the camp meeting, which stressed individualism as much as the need for a disciplining group. The industrial and urban revolutions called the church into the city as a corporate entity as well as in congregational form. The Social Gospel brought an urgency for the denomination to speak as a corporate voice.[7]

A more subtle influence, after the Industrial Revolution of the late 1800s, was a tendency for the denomination to assume the corporate nature of business. This, almost as much as the need to support and coordinate the diverse activities of a growing church, brought general agencies into being. The emergence of special interest groups, including racial and ethnic groups, resulted in struggles for power and influence in the corporate body. What appears to have happened in the meantime is the obscuring of the original emphasis of the church, winning souls to Christ. In its stead has emerged a new "bottom line" which is *to change society by reforming it through collective actions.*

It is instructive to ask laypersons to state the mission of their congregation. A wide variety of answers are given, including, "to increase our membership," "to serve our community," and "to educate our children in the faith." Only occasionally is reference made to the original "bottom line" of our movement—to win others to Christ.

There seems to be a strong conviction of the importance of projecting a good image and having good public relations in order to attract people. In one church, a consultant asked a group of thirty leaders, "Who in this church is responsible to reach the unchurched in the community?" The question was greeted with silence until someone asked, "You mean we're supposed to do that? I thought we just took whoever happened to come in."

Several congregations prefer to use terms such as "church growth committee" or "membership committee" as a substitute for "evangelism." Evidently evangelism makes them uncomfortable.

One local church established a goal of receiving "three new families" during the next year. When the district superintendent asked what criteria were used to settle on that number, he was told, "We need the income from that many families to balance our budget for next year." Winning people to Christ was not their goal.

The *United Methodist Reporter* (January 23, 1981), reporting results of a survey dealing with issues related to the "church growth movement," observed, "issues raised by the 'church growth movement' are not a high priority among the laity of The United Methodist Church." While one cannot equate church growth to winning persons to Christ, there is an obvious relationship between the two.

In recent times many United Methodists have assumed that the church could maintain itself, and perhaps grow, by holding onto its young people and absorbing those who came looking for a church home. The goal of increasing membership has not been widely accepted; sometimes to suggest it as a goal brings charges of playing the "numbers" game. Historically, Methodism has attached a high degree of importance to preaching and worship which result in people being won to Christ, nurtured in his way, and disciplined in love so as to help move toward perfection.

In recent years, however, the church seems to have assumed a corporate character in order to function as a power to change society. One hears that argument in general agency meetings when the propriety of an agency passing resolutions is questioned. As the church has become more structured, its nature has changed. Its increased membership suggested for a while that it was continuing to win people.

During the past decade, however, United Methodism has experienced a decrease in its membership of more than a million members. In spite of this loss, The United Methodist Church remains the third largest religious body in the United States (behind the Roman Catholics and Southern Baptists).[8] This is not because it has concentrated on its basic tenet, winning people, but because it has been an attractive corporate religious giant.[9] People in this nation are eager to be associated with a winner. To many people the logic has been that as long as The United Methodist Church is bigger than others, it has to be better.

The original Methodist societies nurtured and disciplined members, so that they could be witnesses to Christ's power and love. They were not large; they were winners; often they were a persecuted group of people; but they were successful in making an impact on society because the people in those societies were convinced that God worked through them as individuals. That is the power which ignited the denomination!

No organization, religious or otherwise, is immune from the pressures of the social context in which it functions. We have seen that The United Methodist Church has accommodated well to the society of which it is a part. The original concept of its mission has been broadened by a superstructure which not only provides resources for the local churches, but is involved in efforts to change the life of the nation and the denomination. These efforts represent a significant tension area. The polity, as now established, supports the mission of the local church and at the same time focuses attention on efforts to change society through some of its general agencies.

This is not to suggest a return to a theoretically "better" yesterday. Realistically that didn't exist. The question posed is one of polity and evaluation. A major problem is that there is no officially stated or commonly agreed upon "bottom line" or criterion for evaluating our denomination. Thus there is no common understanding in the denomination of what it is to be in mission.

The 1976 *Book of Discipline* contained a paragraph entitled "The Objectives of Mission"[10] as part of the introduction to the chapter on "Administrative Order." The statement, as revised, was intended to be Paragraph 103 of the 1980 *Book of Discipline*. Somehow it was lost in the process of General Conference and never made it to the final version of *The Book of Discipline*. While inclusion in *The Book of Discipline* would not assure consensus about a statement of mission, it would provide a basis for discussion and evaluation. Only when there are clear goals is evaluation possible.

Dealing creatively with tension surrounding historic purposes versus current practices means dealing with such questions as these: What is the "bottom line" for The United Methodist Church? Can we build on a polity based on winning persons to Christ and nurturing them so that their individual and corporate actions reflect

Christian discipleship? Should the focus of polity be support and encouragement of local churches, Annual Conferences and/or the general church? If all of these are appropriate, are they currently in proper balance?

Evaluation Methods

Evaluation is as old as humankind. The first large group of books on evaluation as *a separate field of study*, however, were produced in the early 1970s. The separate discipline of evaluation was spawned by the necessity of dealing with large and complex organizational structures. Today it is possible to subscribe to evaluation journals, attend evaluation workshops, and even major in evaluation as a sub-science at some major universities.

There are several types of evaluation, each of which is used for a particular purpose. Performance appraisal, for example, is used by administrators to measure how well a person carries out certain tasks or fulfills particular roles. Performance analysis usually involves collaborative planning, seeks to identify forces blocking persons or organizational effectiveness, and identifies steps to be taken to diminish the effects of these forces. Organizational effectiveness focuses on the organization as a whole rather than individuals within it. These illustrations indicate only a few of the many varieties of evaluation. Unfortunately, evaluation is often seen primarily as performance appraisal.

Evaluation, with all of its forms, methods, and experts, is an outgrowth of formal planning processes instituted by corporations during the past quarter century. Since the church has emulated corporate business during these years, it is not surprising that formal evaluation procedures have been adopted in general agencies, Annual Conferences, and local churches.

Evaluation of the General Agencies

At the general church level, evaluation is treated as any other corporate activity. It is undertaken with the same motivation and expertise as corporations utilize when they plan and evaluate. Staff persons set goals which are reviewed and approved by the members of the agencies.[11] Task forces and committees are established to develop evaluation models. Staff members, along with elected agency members, then conduct the evaluation.

Program agencies undergo two levels of evaluation. The first is self-evaluation, planned and conducted by the agency itself. The second involves review by the General Council on Ministries' Unit on Evaluation and Coordination. The Council consults with the agency in the development of its self-evaluation plan. The Council's basic concern is whether the agency is carrying out its responsibilities as established by General Conference.

One of the ironies of the evaluation process in corporations and in the general church is that in many cases those who set the goals, decide on evaluative criteria, and are responsible for achieving program results, are the same individuals who do the evaluating. While agency members are reactors and legitimators in the evaluation process, the key determiners of program, evaluation and program results are staff members. Perhaps it could be done differently.

One difficulty faced by agency members in the evaluation process is their limited knowledge of their agency's programs and organization. The process by which they are selected to the membership of the agency favors the election of persons with limited experience in the management of complex organizations. Another complication is the rule, voted by General Conference, which limits the tenure of a member of an agency to eight years. This rule assures that at least 50 percent of the voting members of a general agency will change each quadrennium.[12] Economic pressures have further limited the effectiveness of voting members of general agencies by allowing for fewer meetings. As a result of these limitations, the agencies and the church are effectively dependent on general agency staff for evaluation.

Evaluation of the Local Church

The 1968 General Conference passed legislation directing the local church Charge Conference to evaluate the effectiveness of the local congregation annually.[13] While this direction has not been ignored, it has not been followed with consistent effectiveness, and often only at the insistence of the district superintendent.

On the other hand, evaluation of the performance of individual local church members is limited. Disciplining of members, a method used in earlier Methodist tradition, is evaluation in its strictest sense. Since the time of the Societies, disciplining has been an integral part of individual growth. While it fell in and out of favor over time, personal evaluation is still "on the books."

The most commonly used criteria for evaluating local church members are attendance at worship services and contributions of money. These criteria are applied often by local churches evaluating inactive members during the three-year period of cultivation required by *The Book of Discipline*. It is not common today, however, to find disciplining of local church members comparable to that in the early Societies. In contrast to Asbury's expectations, today one often hears the comment, "Anyone can be a United Methodist." This is more a reflection on the lack of discipline than a statement about the church's inclusiveness.

No attempt is made to evaluate the performance of individual members in the exercise of their ministry.[14] Does this mean that individual members' ministry is unimportant and that the only ministry important enough to be evaluated is that of the pastor? Why has the importance of the individual church member's ministry been ignored?

The size and organization of the church are very different today from early Methodist beginnings. The United Methodist Church today does not consider itself to be a collection of isolated groups of people attempting to be disciplined Christians. It considers itself a church having local congregations who are "in witness and mission" in their communities. Being "in witness and mission" is defined and accomplished differently by each congregation.

Evaluation of the Pastor

Evalution of pastors is swift and direct *in the local church*. A pastor is followed or not followed. People come to worship or they don't. Money is given or it isn't. These are evaluative decisions made by people who are members of local congregations.

However, a more formal process has been legislated. In 1976, General Conference adopted and assigned to the local church Committee on Pastor-Parish Relations the responsibility "to evaluate annually the effectiveness of the minister and staff."[15] In 1980 annual evaluation by this committee and the district superintendent became a requirement for continued guaranteed appointment for the ministers.[16] In addition, evaluation became "a continuous process" for ministerial members of Annual Conferences.[17] These changes emphasize the accountability of ministerial members to the local church and to the denomination.

Annual Conferences are now preparing for local church pastoral evaluation. By late 1981, sixty-six Annual Conferences had sent leaders to pastoral evaluation training events sponsored by the Division of Ordained Ministry of the General Board of Higher Education and Ministry.[18]

The motivations for this evaluation process are: (1) a need to "weed out the incompetency in each of us and those who are incompetent among us,"[19] (2) a fear that the church is falling behind secular society and a desire to encourage pastors to continue to grow through continuing education, and (3) an awareness that present informal evaluation methods, with their unclear criteria, have resulted in confusion and mistrust. Those who initiated this pastoral evaluation program feel that evaluation methods used by district superintendents in the past are inadequate.[20]

The materials being developed include a module for evaluating the effectiveness of the local church as well as

EVALUATION

that of the pastor. Potential conflict may be seen between the Committee on Pastor-Parish Relations and the Administrative Board. By assuming responsibility for goal setting and evaluation of the local church the former may displace the latter.

The process assumes that the district superintendent will (1) be involved in detailed evaluation with about a third of the district churches each year, (2) participate with each local church in designing the evaluation process to be used, (3) receive a summary of and implications from the evaluation results, and (4) respond to the summary annually in writing and periodically in person before the pastor and the local church committee. Since a separate evaluative process will be used by the district superintendent for appointment-making, the local church process should focus on the effectiveness of the pastor's leadership in achieving the local church's goals.

This process will require of the district superintendent, as connectional representative, a heavy commitment of time and an increased number of visits to local churches. The district superintendent will be required to assist local churches in formulating statements of purpose for congregational mission and in clarifying the pastor's priorities in leading the congregation toward accomplishment of its stated mission.[21]

For the first time, laypersons will have a role in supervising itinerant clergy. The process developed by the Division of Ordained Ministry could place the local Committee on Pastor-Parish Relations in a supervisory role over the pastor. Thus, the office of district superintendent could be displaced from its historic role of supervising itinerant clergy.

Evaluation is a function of a supervisor. It would be

natural for persons using the secular supervision model to assume that the authority of the Committee on Pastor-Parish Relations goes beyond verbs such as "confer," "counsel," and "consult," to more directive ones such as "instruct" and "direct."[22] Such an assumption could move United Methodism toward a congregational system of pastoral appointments.

Results

If the "bottom line" of the polity is the historic one of winning people to Christ, The United Methodist Church has not been effective during the last decade. It is impossible to be effective at winning people to Christ and simultaneously experience a membership decline of more than a million persons. An important factor in the United Methodist membership decline between 1964 and 1975 is a sharp drop in the number of persons received on profession of faith. A secondary factor is the slight increase in the number of persons removed by Charge Conference action.[23]

The membership decline occurred not so much because we *lost* people, but because we did not *win* people. During the same period some other denominations had significant membership gains. These statistics reveal a fact whose meaning we cannot ignore. The early Methodist objective of winning people to Christ has not been pursued effectively by the denomination in this generation.

There is no formal process for evaluating the performance of the denomination as a whole. We evaluate the leaders, the general agencies, and the local churches, but these do not add up to United Metho-

EVALUATION

dism. Evaluations of the denomination as a whole are based on membership, attendance, and money. If these are adequate criteria for evaluating the local church they are inadequate criteria for evaluation of the denomination as a whole.

Adequate evaluation is not even attained when we consider whether we have been successful in pursuing a different "bottom line." For example, if the "bottom line" has been to change society utilizing the collective force of a national church structure, we have achieved the formation of the structure,* but it is impossible to measure accurately the effect of this structure on social change. We have no data for using this additional criterion.

These two differing interpretations of the "bottom line" of United Methodism deeply divide members. Evaluation based only on the historic roots in which the polity grew would emphasize the care of souls more than social change, evangelization of the world more than championing equal opportunity, and individual and congregational discipline rather than issuing resolutions as a corporate body. This type of evaluation, based only on our historical roots, would ignore our history as a responsible Christian body during the past two centuries.

There is no question but that evaluation produces some tension and anxiety within the church. Nevertheless, that is not sufficient reason to disregard the need

---

*It is possible now to identify general agencies which have parallels in most other corporations. There are an education group (human relations), a product group (missions), a finance group (in about three locations within the general agencies), a public relations and communications group, a recruitment group (training), and an executive council.

for such evaluation. It is clear that evaluation, accountability, effectiveness, and competence will continue to be concerns of ministers and laypersons alike at all levels within The United Methodist Church. As we move forward into our third century as a denomination, we must continue to search for appropriate evaluation models and tools for assessing our work, for the local church and pastor, for the Annual Conference, and for the denomination as a whole.

CHAPTER 6

The Spirit of United Methodism

One of the characteristics of United Methodists is activity. They don't worry about correct theology or the proper way to do things. They worry about people and their lives. They want to get involved and straighten things out.

This spirit of United Methodism is the essence of what made United Methodism one of the most potent religious forces in the United States. United Methodism did not begin as an established church with an unbending theology and formal structure. Rather, it began and has continued to be a movement of people striving to find a way to bring the message of Jesus Christ to the people who live around them.

Key words describing United Methodism's polity are "pragmatic" and "practical." United Methodist spirit comes from a sense of practicality which has influenced the shape of its polity and its life.

A Practical People

United Methodist polity was developed as Methodist Societies grew into a church. Adjustments were made to meet new situations. For example, no theologian took study leave to create the Articles of Religion which served as the standard doctrine for Methodists. Not at all! John Wesley simply abridged those of the Church of England. The American church adopted them at the 1784 General Conference and has published them in every *Book of Discipline* since 1790. The Evangelical Association and the United Brethren were just as practical—they adapted the Methodist book! The church was too practical and intent on its mission to use its energy to duplicate what was available and adequate for the task.

Methodist polity grew out of the needs and experiences of Societies whose purposes were to win people to Christ, to nurture and discipline them in the faith, and to lead them on to perfection. At the same time, there was need to heal the sick, feed the hungry, clothe the naked, and minister to the oppressed. The Societies and their individual members undertook these ministries as well. Thus, from its earliest days, our church polity charged its members to reach out to change the culture surrounding it.

No organization can endure very long if it does not provide for the second generation of believers. Nor can it grow unless it has an orderly means for overseeing the new parts it generates. In keeping with their practical nature, leaders created the polity needed to accomplish their tasks.

Itinerant ministry, for example, was not a premeditated design of John Wesley. Rather, it was a strategy to help achieve the goal of saving souls.[1] American leaders decided that an itinerant ministry would free pastors to preach the gospel without the entanglements and compromises caused by being rooted in one community. Since the itinerant preachers had no home base, they needed a place to be uplifted, a place of accountability, and a place to belong and feel a oneness with others like themselves. Out of these needs came the Annual Conference. Eventually the General and Jurisdictional Conferences were established to perform specific functions.

The camp meeting, abandoned by the Presbyterians, was appropriated, widely used, and became a Methodist institution.[2] The circuit rider was a practical frontier expression of the itinerant system, a concept later adopted by other denominations. Establishment of the Book Concern was a way to educate traveling clergy who were generally untrained and often anti-intellectual.

Such were the adjustments made to meet the challenge of the American frontier. These innovations were made a part of the hierarchical structure of the church because creative Methodist leaders managed to provide the conferences with a high degree of democratic decision making.

As times and conditions changed, United Methodism's practicality made it experiment with new structures. Its desire for status as well as its involvement in a variety of mission activities resulted in the creation of general agencies. As it shifted from a sectarian movement to a denomination, The United Methodist Church seemed to adopt business and industry structures, thus becoming an organization first and a spiritual entity second.[3]

This change began with the formation of the Missionary Society in 1820. At this point, according to Frederick Norwood, the church first "made a distinction between itself, understood totally as a missionary movement . . . and a special department whose responsibility was mission."[4] This analysis may oversimplify cultural dynamics affecting social organizations during the past half century, but evidence suggests that the United Methodist response to American culture was more adaptation than transformation.[5]

The change from a spiritual movement to an organization has created uncertainty about the "bottom line" of United Methodism. Profit and efficiency, the twin emphases of industry and business structures, are certainly not appropriate. Some United Methodists see as goals in themselves such activities as testing and evaluating clergy, letting each special interest group have a piece of the action, and insisting on widespread participation in decision making. While these endeavors are neither positive nor negative in themselves, the net result of the shift in emphasis is an encouragement not of excellence but of *willingness to settle for mediocrity*.

Nominating general agency voting members is a case in point. The process is complicated, demands compromises, and produces mixed results. In the words of one bishop, "When you finally come up with a slate of nominations, you feel like apologizing to the church." The process trivializes the denomination's valid commitment to provide for widely representative membership on all decision-making bodies. The process places so much emphasis on machinery that it obscures the goal of finding the best people to serve.

One reason for the current emphasis on excellence in ministry is a concern that the current guaranteed appointment system produces and protects mediocrity. Job security inherent in the present system puts a premium on not rocking the boat. Conformity is emphasized. No one is encouraged to deviate from the norm enough to speak up for the spiritual dimension of United Methodism.

United Methodism's practical polity served well in the

past when missional goals and purposes were clear. When mission became unclear, polity tended to become an end in itself. *Many of the tensions we have considered herein are the result not of polity but of a lack of common purpose in mission.*

A Common Purpose

Originally the mission purpose of The United Methodist Church was to bring God's grace to persons, to build strong local units to convert, nurture, and disciple those who would change the world, and to create the structures needed to support and expand that mission. Mission purpose focused on the *roots* of our faith.

We have seen how the mission purpose shifted over the years and divided the church. Recently the mission purpose has been to create a new society within our own organization. Emphasis has been on internal organizational compliance with a few behavioral expectations of our faith. The focus is on the *fruits* of the faith with no corresponding emphasis on the *roots* of the faith!

It is not the aim of this book to prescribe what the mission purpose of the denomination should include. It is our purpose, however, to point out that the polity as originally established supported a particular missional goal. That same polity is now expected to support quite a different type of goal or goals. Since United Methodist polity should be shaped by its function and/or goals, there is little wonder that tensions are being experienced.

If The United Methodist Church is to minister effectively in its third century, *leaders and members must develop, understand, and articulate a clear sense of identity and purpose.* Lack of a common purpose affects all parts of the church—members, leaders, Annual Conferences, and general agencies. As long as the resources of an organization are not united to achieve a common purpose, there will be unrest, internal dissension, drift, and apathy. Ethos, or spirit, is mobilized by a common purpose. A group that shares a commitment to a common purpose is able to move together. This is a spiritual reality. It is a transcendental dimension in life.

The word "mission" is the key. When people have a common mission, they feel together, they trust one another, and they want to be together. Mission grips people and moves them from preoccupation with mundane concerns to sacrificial achievements. It unites them.

Neither connectional structures nor General Conference legislation unify the denomination. Polity is merely a *means* to achieve the mission to which God calls United Methodism. It is time to shift the focus from differences which divide to factors which unify. It is time to focus on those factors in our heritage and experience which can draw us together and hold us together.

The Book of Discipline of 1980 states, "There is . . . general agreement that The United Methodist Church stands urgently in need of doctrinal reinvigoration for the sake of authentic renewal."[6] Developing a common missional purpose is a theological issue. Bishop Roy Short states it well: "There has never been a great revival of religion without a rediscovery of religious trust. The message must get hold of us again."[7]

The current interest in Wesleyan theology may help us discover bases upon which to build a common purpose. We must become informed and trust our historic past which binds us as people. The personal experience of God's grace, the living of disciplined, transformed lives, the press toward perfection and the work of God in transforming lives and communities could be themes for our search.[8]

Formerly, "Methodists found their bond of unity lay 'not in the fine print of our prayer books' but in a 'strange warming of the heart' which was common to all although variously expressed."[9] What is "common to all" today? Perhaps if we explore together, we may discover that people and organizations are not isolated, but intertwined. We may be as surprised as Timothy Smith who found that the Social Gospel and revivalism were direcly related.[10] We may discover anew that we need one another!

Locating the Spirit

The Annual Conference was the ethos-creating agent for the denomination from its early days. Here clergy met to exchange information, share stories, listen to good preaching, and make important decisions about churches they served.

The primary business of the Annual Conference involved ministerial care, ordination, support for institutions, financing the activities of various boards, and conference and denominational mission activities. The primary emphasis of the conference was winning people to Christ, care and nurture of souls, and keeping the church mission in focus for all members. The Annual Conference session was a warm and exciting gathering of persons concerned about their part in the mission of the church, an annual reunion, a source of inspiration and renewal.

Conferences in the past served as a forum for preachers. The conference preacher provided a model for clergy in developing their own preaching. This was once the primary place for revising the preaching model after seminary. Most of all, however, the preaching at the Annual Conference clarified the mission, united the members, and inspired pastors and laypersons to get on with the work. The key preacher was the bishop.

Because its nature had changed, perhaps today the Annual Conference cannot be the place for ethos building. Perhaps cultural and polity changes have made it impossible to recover this historic role.

If Annual Conference sessions cannot be the source of ethos, perhaps the district can fulfill that role. Districts are closer to the local church; pastors as well as laypersons can attend frequent meetings for information and inspiration. Although no tradition exists in the church for such a development, the ingredients are there—connectional leader, local pastors, and laypersons.

The bishops or general agencies could help the church develop its spirit of common purpose. This would necessitate a radical change in agenda for both groups.

Or the spirit might be found in the local church. "It is primarily at the level of the local church that the Church encounters the world."[11] The local church is central to United Methodist polity. It is the source of funds, the supply base of leaders, and the place where the gospel is proclaimed to the world.

It really doesn't matter *where* the common mission

purpose is redeveloped, as long as we reclaim a common purpose! The pressures of death, destruction, famine, misery, and lost hope are on every side. The United Methodist Church, begun among outcasts of English society and carried across America by preachers riding lonely trails to bring the Good News to all people, is called again to speak to a needy world.

When we come together and find renewed vision and purpose, we shall have found the means by which to resolve the tensions in the connection, this connection which binds us together as United Methodists. Built by ordinary, practical people who felt their hearts strangely warmed, The United Methodist Church once again asks such people to unite and witness to the claim of Jesus Christ upon their lives.

Notes

Chapter 1

1. Report of the Committee on Itinerancy of the Council of Bishops to Delegates of the General Conference, 1980. *United Methodism: Conciliar, Connectional, Itinerant.*
2. *Daily Christian Advocate,* April 17, 1980, p. 209.
3. *The Book of Discipline of The United Methodist Church* (Nashville: The United Methodist Publishing House, 1980), Paragraph 15.
4. *Ibid.,* Paragraph 10, Article IV; Paragraph 37, Article II.
5. David C. Shipley, "The European Heritage," in *The History of American Methodism,* 3 vols., ed. Emory Stevens Bucke (Nashville: Abingdon Press, 1964), vol. I, p. 17.
6. *The Book of Discipline,* 1980. See Paragraph 2501.
7. E. Benson Perkins, "Deed of Declaration," in *The Encyclopedia of World Methodism,* 2 vols., ed. Nolan B. Harmon (Nashville: The United Methodist Publishing House, 1974), vol. I, p. 646.
8. *The Book of Discipline,* 1980, Paragraph 210.
9. This principle of the connection was stated by Bishop Ralph T. Alton in an interview on September 5, 1981, in Madison, Wisconsin.
10. For Wesley's reasoning, see Richard M. Cameron, *The Rise of Methodism* (New York: Philosophical Library, 1954), especially pp. 352ff.
11. Nolan B. Harmon and John Kent, "Development of the Presiding Eldership," in *The Encyclopedia of World Methodism,* vol. II, p. 2284.
12. Frank Baker, *From Wesley to Asbury* (Durham, N. C.: Duke University Press, 1976), p. 131.
13. Arthur Bruce Moss, "Methodism in Colonial America," in *The History of American Methodism,* vol. I, pp. 129-30.
14. Winthrop S. Hudson, *Religion in America* (New York: Charles Scribner's Sons, 1965), pp. 126ff.
15. William Warren Sweet, *The Story of Religion in America* (New York: Harper & Brothers, 1950), p. 238.

16. Frederick A. Norwood, "The Church Takes Shape," in *The History of American Methodism,* vol. I, pp. 480ff.
17. *Ibid.,* p. 485.
18. Frederick A. Norwood, *The Story of American Methodism* (Nashville: Abingdon Press, 1974), pp. 113ff.
19. Nolan B. Harmon, "The Organization of the Methodist Episcopal Church, South," in *The History of American Methodism,* vol. II, pp. 86-143.
20. Timothy L. Smith, *Revivalism and Social Reform* (Nashville: Abingdon Press, 1957).

Chapter 2

1. *The Book of Discipline,* 1980, Paragraph 439.
2. *Ibid.,* Paragraph 437.
3. Norwood, *The Story of American Methodism,* p. 36.
4. Martin Rist, "Methodism Goes West," in *The History of American Methodism,* vol. II, pp. 420-68.
5. *Ibid.,* pp. 466-67.
6. Cameron, *The Rise of Methodism,* pp. 352ff.
7. Walter W. Benjamin and Leland Scott, "The Methodist Episcopal Church in the Postwar Era," in *The History of American Methodism,* vol. II, pp. 315-90.
8. John O. Gross, "The Field of Education," in *The History of American Methodism,* vol. III, p. 243.
9. Murray H. Leiffer, *Changing Expectations and Ethics in the Professional Ministry* (Evanston, Ill.: Garrett Theological Seminary, 1969), especially pp. 124ff.
10. Information provided by Rosalie Bentzinger, Division of Diaconal Ministry, 1981.
11. *The Book of Discipline,* 1980, Paragraphs 517-522.
12. *Ibid.,* Paragraph 437.
13. For a detailed description of the current process of appointment-making, see *The Book of Discipline,* 1980, Paragraphs 527-531.
14. Norwood, *The Story of American Methodism,* pp. 138ff.
15. *The Book of Discipline,* 1968, Paragraphs 4, 107, 662, 814.1.
16. *The Book of Discipline,* 1972, Paragraph 391.
17. *The Book of Discipline,* 1976, Paragraph 527.
18. *The Book of Discipline,* 1980, Paragraph 527.
19. Woodie White in telephone interview on January 18, 1982.
20. *Ethnic Minorities in The United Methodist Church* (Nashville: Discipleship Resources, 1976), p. 1.
21. *The Book of Discipline,* 1980, Paragraph 68, Article XV; Paragraphs 248.8, 251.

22. White, telephone interview.
23. *Ibid.*
24. Survey information provided by Dr. Woodie White.
25. From reports of Annual Conference sessions in *Newscope* during May and June, 1981.

Chapter 3

1. Dr. Alvin Lingren and Bishop Ralph T. Alton believe such challenges are increasing. Since these cases ultimately are taken to civil court, not the Judicial Council, no official record exists of their number.
2. Paul A. Mickey and Robert L. Wilson, *Denominational Decision Making* (Durham, N. C.: The J. M. Ormond Center, The Divinity School, Duke University, 1979). In their analysis of decision making at the 1976 General Conference these authors point out that General Conference delegates are not responsible to represent the people who elect them, pp. 9, 10.
3. Nolan B. Harmon, "Structural and Administrative Changes," in *The History of American Methodism*, vol. III, pp. 8-10.
4. Norwood, *The Story of American Methodism*, p. 144.
5. *The Doctrines and Discipline of The Methodist Church* (Nashville: The Methodist Publishing House, 1940), p. 99.
6. *The Book of Discipline*, 1980, Paragraph 267.
7. William R. Cannon, "Education, Publication, Benevolent Work and Missions," in *The History of American Methodism*, vol. I, p. 572.
8. Ben Primer, *Protestants and American Business Methods* (Ann Arbor: University of Michigan Press, 1979), p. 4.
9. *Daily Christian Advocate*, February 15, 1980, p. D84.
10. This understanding of the current place of the Annual Conference was expressed by Bishop W. McFerrin Stowe in an interview on December 10, 1981, in Dallas, Texas.
11. See Robert L. Wilson, "Where Did All the Money Go?" Research Information Bulletin 78-3 for an analysis of United Methodist expenditures for 1967-76.
12. *The United Methodist Reporter*, November 6, 1981, p. 3.
13. *The Book of Discipline*, 1980, Paragraphs 248-251, 266.1, 441.

Chapter 4

1. Jerry W. Robinson, Jr., and Roy A. Clifford, *Leadership Roles in Community Groups* (Urbana: University of Illinois Press, 1975), pp. 2, 3.

2. *Daily Christian Advocate*, April 27, 1976, Advance Edition F, "Bishop and District Superintendent Study Commission 1972-76," p. 13.
3. *Ibid.*
4. This symbolic leadership role of bishops was expressed by some clergy, laypersons, and a group of seminary students interviewed at Garrett-Evangelical Seminary, Evanston, Ill., November 13, 1981.
5. Baker, *From Wesley to Asbury*, p. 8.
6. *Ibid.*, p. 12.
7. *The Study of the General Superintendency of the Methodist Church*, A Report to the General Conference of 1964, p. 119.
8. *The Doctrines and Discipline of The Methodist Church*, 1939, p. 11.
9. J. Bruce Behney and Paul H. Eller, *The History of the Evangelical United Brethren Church* (Nashville: Abingdon Press, 1979), p. 190.
10. *Daily Christian Advocate*, 1976, pp. F-16-17.
11. Walter N. Vernon, "The Growing Tribalism of United Methodism," *The Circuit Rider*, 3 (May 1979), p. 17.
12. Murray H. Leiffer, "United Methodism, 1940-60," in *The History of American Methodism*, vol. III, p. 513ff.
13. Norwood, *The Story of American Methodism*, p. 414.
14. Leiffer in *The History of American Methodism*, p. 518ff.
15. Norwood, *The Story of American Methodism*, p. 414.
16. James McGregor Burns, *Leadership* (New York: Harper & Row, 1978), pp. 452ff.
17. *Ibid.*, p. 455.
18. *Ibid.*
19. Kristine M. and Bruce A. Rogers, *Paths to Transformation* (Nashville: Abingdon Press, 1982).
20. Norwood, *The Story of American Methodism*, p. 67.
21. *The Doctrines and Discipline of The Methodist Episcopal Church*, 1872, Paragraph 76.
22. Norwood, *The Story of American Methodism*, p. 132.

Chapter 5

1. *The Book of Discipline*, 1980, Paragraph 101.
2. *The Book of Discipline*, 1968, Paragraph 145.
3. *The Book of Discipline*, 1976, Paragraph 1005.18. See also *The Book of Discipline*, 1980, Paragraph 802.
4. Baker, *From Wesley to Asbury*, p. 122.
5. See Leiffer, "United Methodism, 1940-60," in *The History of American Methodism*, vol. III, pp. 518-20.
6. One of the first agencies of Methodism was the Mission Board

formed partly to make certain churches were established. W. Richey Hogg, "The Missions of American Methodism," in *The History of American Methodism*, vol. III, pp. 59-128.
7. Jaroslav J. Pelikan, "Methodism's Contribution to America," in *The History of American Methodism*, vol. III, pp. 596-614.
8. Constant H. Jacquet, Jr., ed., *Yearbook of American and Canadian Churches, 1981* (Nashville: Abingdon Press, 1981).
9. As Pelikan suggests, it reflects American culture.
10. *The Book of Discipline*, 1976, Paragraph 801.
11. Leiffer in *The History of American Methodism*, pp. 516-18.
12. *The Book of Discipline*, 1980, Paragraph 810.3.
13. *The Book of Discipline*, 1968, Paragraph 145.
14. *The Book of Discipline*, 1980, Paragraphs 101-106 contain a description of the ministry of all believers.
15. *The Book of Discipline*, 1976, Paragraph 260.2, $d(3)$.
16. *The Book of Discipline*, 1980, Paragraph 423.1*b*.
17. *The Book of Discipline*, 1980, Paragraph 427.
18. The Rev. Richard Yeager, a staff member of the Divison of Ordained Ministry, provided much of the information relating to evaluation in an interview taped November 20, 1981, in Nashville.
19. *Ibid.*
20. *Ibid.*
21. *The Book of Discipline*, 1980, Paragraph 518.1. This provision has been a part of the *Discipline* since 1976.
22. *The Book of Discipline*, 1980, Paragraph 266.2. These are the key verbs describing the relationship of the committee to the pastoral staff. Evaluate is a recent legislative addition and opens up the possibility of a more directive relationship.
23. Warren J. Hartman, *Membership Trends* (Nashville: Discipleship Resources, 1981), pp. 3-9.

Chapter 6

1. E. Dale Dunlap, "The United Methodist System of Itinerant Ministry: Its Nature and Future," *Occasional Papers*, 30 (January 15, 1980), 2.
2. William Warren Sweet, *Revivalism in America* (New York: Charles Scribner's Sons, 1945), pp. 129, 130.
3. H. Richard Neibuhr, *The Social Sources of Denominationalism* (New York: World Publishing Co., 1962).
4. Norwood, *The Story of American Methodism*, p. 177.
5. Jaroslav J. Pelikan, "Methodism's Contribution to America," in *The History of American Methodism*, vol. III, pp. 596-614. See also F. Gerald Ensley, "American Methodism: An Experiment in

Secular Christianity," in *The History of American Methodism,* vol. III, pp. 623-26.
6. *The Book of Discipline,* 1980, Paragraph 67.
7. Bishop Roy H. Short, in an interview in Nashville on November 21, 1981.
8. Neal F. Fisher, *Context for Discovery* (Nashville: Abingdon Press, 1981), pp. 120ff for some elaboration on these motifs.
9. Walter W. Benjamin, "The Methodist Episcopal Church in the Postwar Era," in *The History of American Methodism,* vol. II, p. 319.
10. Smith, *Revivalism and Social Reform,* pp. 7-10.
11. *The Book of Discipline,* 1980, Paragraph 202.